Getting Started
in Options

Also available from John Wiley & Sons

Getting Started in Options

Second Edition

Michael C. Thomsett

JOHN WILEY & SONS, INC.

New York • Chichester • Brisbane • Toronto • Singapore

In recognition of the importance of preserving what has been written, it is a policy of John Wiley & Sons, Inc., to have books of enduring value printed on acid-free paper, and we exert our best efforts to that end.

This publication is designed to provide accurate and authoritative information in regard to the subject matter covered. It is sold with the understanding that the publisher is not engaged in rendering legal, accounting, or other professional service. If legal advice or other expert assistance is required, the services of a competent professional person should be sought. From a *Declaration of Principles jointly adopted by a Committee of the American Bar Association and a Committee of Publishers.*

Library of Congress Cataloging-in-Publication Data:

Thomsett, Michael C.
    Getting started in options / by Michael C. Thomsett.—2nd ed.
        p.   cm.
    Includes index.
    ISBN 0-471-57974-2 (paper)
    1. Stock options.   I. Title.
HG6042.T46   1993
332.63'228—dc20   92-23547

Printed in the United States of America

10   9   8   7   6   5

Contents

Getting Started
in Options

Introduction: An Investment with Many Faces

S ome types of investment are widely recognized and understood by most people. This is because there is a general acceptance or sense of legitimacy about them. The stock market and real estate, for example, are well understood by just about everyone—even to the point that very real risks might be ignored or overlooked in some instances. Or, if these forms of investing are not truly familiar, there may at least be the belief that they are known, and that risks are small.

Understanding makes it much easier for new investors to enter specific markets. Real estate is known for its historical appreciation and safety. And the stock market is the most popular way to invest, either through direct ownership of shares or through purchases of shares in mutual funds.

Those markets are popular because they are understood by the investing public. And by the same argument, an investment that is *not* well understood creates a problem in the mind of the investor. It may be thought of as too risky, requiring too

1

much capital, or too exotic for mainstream tastes and preferences. Along with the lack of comfort, risks may be overestimated or exaggerated in some instances.

The options market is widely misunderstood in this way. Lack of understanding creates fear. What do you think about when the word *options* is spoken? Some equate options with complexity and risk, and reject this alternative as being appropriate only for the speculator. But that is not necessarily true. Options may be highly speculative *or* highly conservative, depending on the specific strategies employed. In some cases, options can be used to hedge a position or to provide protection against loss. You will be able to overcome the apprehension of a new idea by gaining knowledge about it and then making an informed judgment.

If, upon gaining information, you decide that options are not right for you, at least that is an informed judgment. On the other hand, a rejection of any form of investment without first gaining a preliminary understanding of how it works would exclude the possibility that it might be beneficial to you.

Options first began trading publicly in 1973. Unlike the stock market, this is a relatively short-term performance history, so it is difficult to compare options with longer-term institutions. We cannot see how options investors or speculators might have fared in the stock market crash of 1929, or how they might have come through the bull market of the 1950s. If your parents have owned stocks over many years, chances are that their experiences have influenced your attitudes about that market. It is less likely that your parents have had many years' experience buying and selling options.

Options today serve a number of different purposes. This book is concerned with the strategic uses of stock options that are traded publicly, either for speculation or for one of a number of other uses. On the most speculative side, options are pure risks and gambles on a stock's movement. On the other end of the spectrum, options are employed to insure against losses by hedging risk positions. There are a range of possible strategies in between these extremes. To decide how you can profit in the options market—or if options are even appropriate in your case—you need to go through a four-step process of evaluation:

1. Master the terminology of this highly specialized and complex market. The language of options may be foreign to even the seasoned stock market investor or expert—because so many ideas not common to stocks are constantly at work in the options market.

2. Identify and recognize the risk profile associated with each type of option investment. Many different investors and speculators use a broad range of strategies involving options. As you might imagine, that also means that the range of risk is broad. You will need to determine whether you belong in the conservative camp or the speculative camp before deciding whether to use options in a particular manner.

3. Observe the market. Watch how option values change in reaction to the broader markets. What factors besides stock prices influence the value of options? When does time work for you and when does it work against you? Once you appreciate the benefits, consequences, and risks of each strategy, you can proceed with confidence.

4. Set a standard for yourself. This is most critical for any form of investing. Without a goal, how can you know when to buy or sell, why you are investing, or even whether a product or strategy has a place in your portfolio? Everything defined by your strategy will define how you make decisions as an investor and, ultimately, whether you succeed or fail.

You can apply this four-part process to all forms of investing, regardless of the market. Even buying shares of stock requires the same steps. Successful investing depends on first gaining knowledge, then identifying risks, tracking the market, and setting your own standards for risk and safety.

You have a tremendous advantage over the option investor and speculator of the mid-1970s. Today, relatively inexpensive computer programs and modems give you affordable on-line access to the trading floor of the stock exchange. If you don't have a computer, your broker certainly has up-to-the-minute access during the trading day, and many brokerage firms now allow you to place orders 24 hours a day.

In the not so distant past, all forms of stock market investment were relatively remote. Investors had to depend on brokers; on especially busy days, your call might not even get through. Brokers had to depend on technology that was not as well developed as today's. They also traded in a new territory, the options market, that was understood by only a small minority of individuals. Today, the market is growing in popularity and in application. You are not alone.

Your broker should be completely versed in options if you are seeking advice. And if you use a discount broker, you should know exactly what you are doing. Even if you work directly with a full-commission broker, you should still have the knowledge to intelligently manage your options strategy and portfolio. A broker's advice may be sound, but you should be willing to take responsibility for your decisions in this market.

This book is designed as an introduction to the options market. It does not recommend that everyone should become a player of the game, or that options are always right or best for everyone. The following chapters explain the terminology and various strategies you can employ in this market; ultimately, you need to decide whether options can enhance your portfolio's profits.

Each chapter includes step-by-step, complete explanations of terminology, accompanied by examples of how those words and phrases affect you as an options investor. The various strategies for conservative and speculative investing are then explained in depth through the use of case histories, examples, illustrations, and identification of different risk profiles.

In many instances, the discussion includes cost, sales price, and profit but excludes mention of a brokerage commission. In reality, you will pay a commission each and every time you buy or sell, in the same way you are charged a fee for buying or selling stocks. But because the amount varies greatly from one broker to another, the details of a brokerage commission or transaction fee are excluded. When you begin calculating your own profit level or breakeven point, be sure to include an allowance for fees and expenses on both sides of the transaction.

In order for any strategy to work, it must be appropriate and comfortable for you. No one idea can work for all investors, and options are no exception to this rule. No matter how practical or foolproof an idea sounds in theory, it should be both profitable and enjoyable for you. Too many would-be investors make their decisions on the advice of others without first investigating on their own. They forget the importance of research, comparison, and analysis, actions to be taken in your own best interests.

You will have the best chances for success by first gathering all of the facts needed to draw an intelligent conclusion. Mere profit is not worth the effort when it comes at the expense of your peace of mind and satisfaction. Real success in the market is a combination of personal accomplishment and financial gain. This book's purpose is to give you the basic information needed to evaluate options and their possible application in your portfolio. By applying the information to your own situation, you will have mastered one of the many possible avenues to becoming a successful and knowledgeable investor.

CHAPTER 1

Calls and Puts

There are basically only two types of investments: equity and debt. Most would agree with this premise. An equity investment is part ownership in something of value, such as shares in a corporation's stock. When you buy shares, you are buying a piece of the company. A bond, however, is an example of a debt instrument. When you purchase a bond, you are loaning your money to the issuer.

When you buy shares of stock, you decide how long to hold and when to sell. Stocks have tangible value in that they represent partial ownership in a corporation. Stockholders are entitled to dividends and will benefit from future profits and appreciation in value of the stock, often over many years. And stocks can be transferred to others or used as collateral to borrow money. These features are widely accepted and understood. But would you be willing to invest money in something that has no tangible value and that you know will be worthless in less than one year? To make the question even more interesting, let's assume that the value of this investment will decline just because time is going by. These are some of the features associated with options that make them appear, at least at first glance, to be pretty risky investments.

These features of options make them especially difficult for many people to accept. You will discover, though, that there may be sound reasons to invest in them. Even the most conservative investor will discover option strategies that can protect their portfolio from loss.

option: the right to buy or sell 100 shares of stock at a fixed price and by a specified date

An *option* is the right to execute a stock transaction. When you own an option, you do not own the stock of the company, only the right to buy or to sell 100 shares of stock. Each option allows you to make the decision to buy or to sell that 100 shares, although restrictions of time do apply. The right to buy or sell is yours for as long as you own the option and for as long as the option exists, which is nine months or less. The option is a finite right that lasts only until the specified date.

There are two types of options. The first is the *call* option, which grants the owner the right to buy 100 shares of stock in the company on which the option is given. It's as though someone else tells the call buyer, "I will allow you to buy 100 shares of this stock, at a specified price per share, any time between now and a date in the future. For that privilege, I want you to pay me a price."

call: an option acquired by a buyer or granted by a seller to buy 100 shares of stock at a fixed price

That price, of course, is determined by how attractive an offer you are given. If the price per share is a good one—based on today's stock price—the cost will be higher. The value of the option can also increase if the stock's price changes in the desired direction. Or it will decrease if the stock changes in the wrong direction. If you buy a call option, you are hoping that the price of the stock will increase. If that happens while you own the option, your option will go up in value along with the stock.

put: an option acquired by a buyer or granted by a seller to sell 100 shares of stock at a fixed price

A *put* is the second type of option. It grants the owner the right to sell 100 shares of stock in the company on which the option is given. It's as though someone tells the put buyer, "I will allow you to sell 100 shares of this stock, at a specified price per share, any time between now and a date in the future. For that privilege, I want you to pay me a price."

Remember, the buyer of a call option hopes the price of the stock will rise. If that happens, the call becomes more valuable. The put buyer believes the price of the stock will fall. If that happens, the put will become increasingly more valuable as the stock's price falls.

If the option buyer—dealing in either calls or puts—is right about the direction the stock's price changes, and if those price movements occur *when* the option investor thinks they will, a profit will result. This is a critical point. Remember, the option is a finite instrument. It will cease to exist within a few months, so time is the determining factor as to whether the option buyer makes or loses money.

Why does the option's value change when the stock's price moves? First of all, the option is only a right, not an instrument in any tangible sense. It is a right related to a specific stock at a specific value, and is good only for a limited amount of time. Consequently, if the timing is off in the purchase of a call or put, the option buyer will not be able to earn a profit.

When you purchase a call, you assume the position, "I am willing to pay the price asked in order to acquire a right. That right will allow me to buy 100 shares of the stock at the indicated fixed price per share at some point in the near future." If the stock's price rises above the fixed price in the option contract, the call becomes more valuable. Imagine a stock's price climbing to $95 per share when you have the right (the option) to buy 100 shares at a price of $80 per share. You can buy 100 shares at $15 per share below market.

The same argument applies to the put buyer, but with the stock moving in the opposite direction. When you buy a put, you are assuming the position, "I am willing to pay the asked price to acquire a right. That right allows me to sell 100 shares of the indicated stock at a fixed price at some time in the near future." If the stock's price falls below the fixed price, the put option gains in value. Imagine holding a put option at $80 per share on a stock for which the current price per share has fallen to $70. You can sell 100 shares at $10 per share above the current price.

THE CALL OPTION

A call is the right to buy 100 shares of stock at a fixed price per share and within a limited period of time. As a call *buyer*, you acquire that right, and as a call *seller*, you grant the right to someone else. (See Figure 1.1.)

Calls are not unique to the stock market. They are used in many situations, although they are not always referred to as calls.

buyer: an investor who purchases a call or a put option (If the value of the option rises, the buyer will realize a profit by selling the option at a price above the purchase price.)

seller: an investor who sells an option (If the value of the option falls, the buyer will realize a profit by buying, or canceling, the option at a price below the original sales price.)

Example: The owner of a house leases it to a tenant under terms known as a lease with the option to buy. A monthly payment includes two parts: rent and a partial deposit toward a future down payment. The future price of the home is fixed at $95,000, but it must be purchased within three years. If the tenant decides not to buy the house, the accumulated deposit will be returned to him. So long as the option is in effect, the owner cannot raise the agreed-upon price.

Three years later, real estate prices have risen dramatically, and the market value of the house is estimated at $110,000, or $15,000 higher than the agreed price. So the owner approaches the tenant

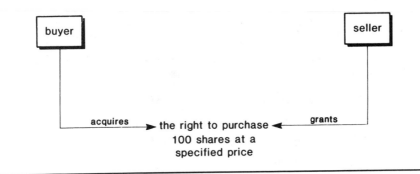

Figure 1.1.   The call option.

with an offer: "I'd like to cancel your option to buy.
I will return your accumulated deposit and add an
extra $7,000 if you will agree to cancel." The tenant
responds, "I am still interested in buying the house
for $95,000. If I go somewhere else, I'll have to pay
$110,000. So I will allow you to cancel our
agreement, but only if you're willing to pay me
$12,000."

This type of option can be negotiated between
the owner (seller of the option) and the tenant (pur-
chaser of the option). Because the underlying prop-
erty has increased in value, the option has also
become a valuable asset. If the buyer and tenant
can agree on a price, the option will be canceled.
Otherwise, the tenant has the right to purchase the
house for $95,000.

Listed options—those traded publicly over the
New York, Chicago, Pacific, American, and Philadelphia stock exchanges—are not negotiated in the
same way. Prices are established strictly by the auc-
tion market, under the same principles that govern
the buying and selling of stocks. An increase in
demand causes prices to rise, and a decrease causes
them to fall. So *market value* is the price that buyers
are willing to pay and sellers are willing to receive.

market value:
the value of an
investment as of a
specified time or
date, or the price
that buyers are
willing to pay and
sellers are willing
to receive for a
stock or option

Under this system, a call buyer or seller will always have a ready market and will be able to cancel an option *contract* at the current market price.

How Call Buying Works

contract: *a single option, including the attributes of that option: identification of the stock on which it is written, the cost of the option, date the option will expire, and the fixed price at which the stock will be bought or sold if the option is exercised*

As the owner of a call, you are not obligated to buy the stock. You have until the *expiration date* of the option to decide what action to take. This decision will depend on movement in the stock's market value.

1. If the market value of the *underlying stock* rises, the option's market value will also rise. So you can either buy the stock at the fixed price per share, which is to *exercise* the option or sell the call for a higher price. In either event, you make a profit. The fixed price of the stock is referred to as the *striking price* of the option.

expiration date: *the date that an option becomes worthless (Every option contract includes a specified date in the future on which it expires.)*

Example: Two months ago, you bought a call at a price of $200, entitling you to buy 100 shares of stock at a price of $55 per share. The option expires later this month. The stock is currently selling at $60 per share, and the option's current price is $600. You have two choices. First, you can exercise the option, buying 100 shares at the agreed price of $55 per share, which is $5 per share below current market value. Or second, you can sell the call for $600, realizing a profit of $400 on the investment.

underlying stock *(also called underlying security): the stock on which the option grants rights to buy or sell (Every stock option refers to a specific, underlying stock.)*

2. If the market value of the stock does not change, you must decide whether to sell the call before its expiration date (after which the option will be worthless) or to hold onto it (hoping the stock's value will rise before the expiration date). The option is a *wasting asset*. If the market value of the stock does not change during the time you own the call, the option will eventually lose its value. The *premium*—the current market value of the option—near expiration will be lower than it was at the time you purchased it.

Example: A few months ago you purchased a call at a price of $500, hoping the stock would increase in value. It will expire later this month but, contrary to your expectations, the stock's price fell. Your call is now worth only $100. You can sell and take your loss of $400, or you can hold on, hoping for a last-minute surge in the stock's market price. However, if you don't take action by the expiration date, the call will become worthless.

3. If the market value of the stock falls, the call will also decline in value. If the drop in the stock's price is substantial, your call option will be worth much less than the price you paid. You can sell and accept only a small part of your original premium or allow the option to expire worthless.

Example: You purchased a call four months ago, paying a premium of $300. You expected the stock's value to rise, meaning the call's value would have risen as well. But the stock's market price fell and the option's value followed and is worth only $100 today. You have a choice: Either sell the call for $100 and accept a $200 loss, or hold onto the option until just before the expiration date, hoping for a last-minute surge in the stock's price. It could happen, although you will also risk further deterioration in the option's value. If you wait beyond the expiration date, the option will be worthless.

Buying a call is risky. Because it has only a limited life, you could lose the entire amount spent

exercise: the act of buying or selling stock at the fixed price specified in the option contract (When a buyer exercises an option, he or she purchases stock at a price lower than market value; when a put is exercised, he or she sells stock at a price higher than market value.)

striking price: the price of stock indicated in the option contract (For example, when an option specifies a striking price of $45 per share, regardless of the actual market value of the stock, that option can be exercised at the striking price of $45 per share.)

wasting asset:
any asset that will
decline in value
over time (An
option is a wasting
asset because it
will be worth its
intrinsic value on
expiration day and
worthless after
expiration day.)

premium: the
current price of an
option, which
buyers pay and
sellers receive at
the time of the
transaction (The
amount is
expressed as the
amount per share,
without dollar
signs; for example,
when a broker
states that an
option "is at 3,"
that means its
premium is $300.)

for the purchase. But it does allow you to benefit from rising prices without requiring you to invest a large sum of money.

Example: You purchased a call last month and spent $100. The current price of the stock is $80 per share. For your $100 investment, you control 100 shares with a total market value of $8,000. Even if the stock falls far below the current price of $80 per share, your risk is limited. The most you can lose is $100, the premium you paid to purchase the call.

Pricing of options depends on the current market value of the stock with regard to the features of the call itself. The pricing of calls is explained later in this chapter.

Example: You gain control of 100 shares of stock selling for $80 per share by purchasing a single call. Buying the stock would cost you $8000, but buying a call costs much less.

You invest much less money, but stand to gain the same amount if the stock rises. You also reduce the risk of loss, because you can never lose more than the price of the call itself.

Example when the stock price rises: You buy a call for $200, which gives you the right to buy 100 shares of stock at $80 per share. If the stock's market value rises above $80, your call will then rise almost dollar for dollar with the stock. So if the stock goes up $4, to $84 per share, your call rises $4 per option as well, and you can earn a profit of $400. That's the same profit you would have realized by investing $8,000 to buy 100 shares.

Example when the stock price falls: You buy a call for $200, which gives you the right to buy 100 shares of stock at $80 per share. By the expiration date of the option, that stock has fallen to only $68 per share. You lose your $200 investment. However, if you had bought 100 shares, your loss at this point would be $1200 (cost of $80 per share, less current value of $68). Compared to buying the stock directly, your option risks are smaller. Your main disadvantage is the time limit. A stockholder has the right to hold those shares indefinitely and to wait for the price to rise again. As an option buyer, you have only a few months to realize a profit.

If a significant drop in price is temporary, the stockholder can afford to wait. During that time, the stockholder is also entitled to dividends that might be declared by the company. And the stock can be pledged as collateral in a brokerage margin account to buy additional shares.

The real advantage of buying calls is that you are not required to deposit a large sum of money, and yet you control the same number of shares. Your losses are limited, but only during the period of the option's life.

How Call Selling Works

A call seller grants, or gives away, the right to buy 100 shares. As a call seller, you receive a payment for granting that right, but must be willing to actually sell 100 shares at a fixed price. This approach to the options market has much greater risks.

As a buyer, the decision to hold, sell, or exercise the option is yours. But as a seller, someone else will make the decision. Sellers will make or lose money in one of the following ways.

1. If the market value of the stock rises, the call also becomes more valuable. The buyer might exercise the option, which means that he or she will "call" 100 shares of stock at the agreed fixed price. You would have to deliver those shares.

Example: You sell a call for 100 shares at $40 per share. A month later, the market value of that stock is $46 per share. If the buyer exercises the option, you will be obligated to deliver 100 shares at $6 below current market value. If you own those shares, you must give them up at the fixed price of $40 each.

Example: Given the same circumstances, you are obligated to deliver 100 shares but do not own them. You will be required to buy them at today's price ($46 per share) and then give them up at the agreed fixed price ($40 per share)—for a loss of $600.

2. If the market value of the stock remains at approximately the same level, the value of the call declines over time because it is a wasting asset. You can cancel the option by buying it at a lower price than you paid. This action results in a profit for you.

Example: You sell a call and receive payment of $400. Several months later, the stock is at about the same value as the option's fixed price, and the option is worth only $100. You can cancel the option by buying it and realize a profit of $300. Or you can allow it to expire worthless, in which case the entire sales price of $400 is a profit to you.

3. If the market value of the stock falls, the option also declines in value. You can either wait until expiration, when the call will expire worthless (meaning you keep the entire amount you received as a seller), or you can cancel the call by buying it and also make a profit.

Example: You sell a call and receive payment of $500. The stock falls far below the option's fixed price and a recovery seems unlikely. If the stock's market value is still at or below the fixed price of the call at the time of expiration, the entire $500 is profit. Or you can cancel your obligation as a seller by buying the contract at its current price. In that case, the difference between your initial sales price and the current buying price is your profit.

How can you sell something before you buy it? The call seller executes the transaction in a way that, to most people, is backward. You understand a transaction involving a purchase, followed by a sale. But the process can also work in reverse. The same technique can be used for selling stocks directly. For example, an investor, expecting prices to fall, instructs a broker to sell 100 shares of stock he does not own. In this technique, known as short selling, he "borrows" the stock from the broker to sell at an anticipated lower price. If correct, he can later cancel the position by buying the shares at the lower price. But if he's wrong, he can only cancel the "short sale" by buying the shares at a higher price than at the time of the original sale.

Short sales occur outside of the stock market every day. Some examples are as follows:

- An art dealer sells limited edition prints, but has only one print that she shows customers. After sales are made, she orders and pays for more prints and then delivers them to the purchasers.
- A car dealer fixes the price of a car with special features that has not yet been manufactured.
- A contractor sells hundreds of tract homes by showing a model before the homes for sale have been built.

short position:
the status of any investment that has been sold and is currently held, pending an offsetting purchase (to cancel the position) or expiration

long position:
the status of any investment that has been bought and is currently held, pending an offsetting sale (to cancel the position) or expiration

When you sell an option, you are said to be in a *short position*. In comparison, a buyer assumes a *long position*.

THE PUT OPTION

A put is the opposite of a call. It is the right to sell 100 shares of stock at a fixed price per share and within a limited period of time. As a put buyer, you acquire that right, and as a put seller, you grant the right to someone else. (See Figure 1.2.)

Buying and Selling Puts

Buyers of puts expect the underlying stock to fall in value. If the stock's market value does fall, the put's value will increase, and if the stock rises, the put's value decreases. As a put buyer, you will have three possible outcomes.

1. If the market value of the stock rises, the value of the put falls in response. You can either sell the put for a lower price and take a loss or hold onto it (hoping the stock will fall before the expiration date).

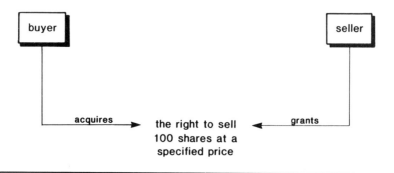

Figure 1.2.   The put option.

Example: You purchased a put two months ago and paid a premium of $200. You expected the price of the stock to fall and, if you had been right, the put's value would have risen. However, the stock's market value rose, with the consequence that the put's value declined. It is now valued at only $25. You have a choice: Sell the put and accept a loss of $175, or hold onto the put, hoping the stock's market value will fall prior to expiration. If you hold the put beyond the expiration date, it will become worthless.

2. If the market value of the stock stays at approximately the same value as when the put was bought, the value of the put falls over time since it is a wasting asset. The closer it is to expiration, the less is its value. You can either sell the put and take a partial loss or hold onto it (hoping the stock's market value will fall before expiration of your put).

Example: You bought a put three months ago and paid a premium of $400. Your expectation: that the stock's market price would fall and, as a result, the put's value would rise. However, expiration is coming up this month, and the stock's market price is about the same as it was when you bought the put. That put has declined in value and is now worth only $100. Your choice is to cash in the put for $100, accepting a $300 loss, or hold onto the put until just before expiration, hoping the stock's price will fall and the put will gain last-minute value.

3. If the market value of the stock falls, the put's value increases. You may either hold onto the put (hoping for further stock declines and more profits from buying the put) or sell it and take a profit. You also have the right to sell 100 shares of stock before expiration at the fixed price, which is higher than current market value.

Example: You bought a put last month and paid a $50 premium. Meanwhile, the stock's market price has fallen to $7 per share below the fixed price specified in the option contract. The put is now valued at $750. You have three choices in this situation. First, you can sell the option and realize a $700 profit on your $50 investment. Second, you can hold onto the put, hoping for further declines in the stock's market price (and, as a result, more profit in the put investment). However, you risk losing part or all of the profit in the event the stock's market price rises. And third, you can exercise the option and sell 100 shares of stock at the specified price, $700 higher than the current market price.

Example: You bought 100 shares of stock a few months ago, paying $38 per share. You are worried about the threat of a falling market; however, you also want to keep the stock. To protect against falling prices, you recently bought a put option and paid a premium of $50. The put grants you the right to sell 100 shares at $40 per share. Then the price of the stock did fall, to $33 per share. The value of the put increases to $750, offsetting the paper loss in the stock. You can sell the option and take your $700 profit, wiping out the loss in the stock. You can also exercise the option, selling the 100 shares of stock at $40 per share, or $7 per share above the current market value. Or, you can hold off taking any action, in case a further price decline occurs in the stock. The put can always be sold before expiration, but declines in the stock price will be offset by increases in the option's price. Your stock position is protected until the put expires.

Rather than buying puts in the hope that stock

prices will fall, you can also be a put seller. Under this plan, you grant someone else the right to sell 100 shares of stock to you at a fixed price. At the time you sell, you receive a premium equal to the put's current market value. Like the call seller, you do not have as much control over the outcome of your investment, since the buyer will decide whether to exercise the put you sold him or her.

Example: Last month, you sold a put with a striking price of 50 ($50 per share). The premium was $250, and you received that amount at the time of the sale. Since that time, the stock's market price has remained in a narrow range between $48 and $53. It is currently at $51 per share. You don't expect the stock's price to fall below the striking price of 50. So long as the market value of the stock remains at or above that price, the put will not be exercised (that is, someone else sells it and forces you to buy 100 shares of stock at 50). If your speculation is correct and the stock's price remains at or above 50, you will make a profit. Your risk is that the stock's price *will* decline before expiration, and you will then be forced to buy shares. You can cancel the contract by buying the put at any time, or you can wait for it to expire. The strategy of selling puts makes sense so long as you believe that the striking price is a reasonable price for the stock—regardless of the market price.

Example: You sold a put with a striking price of 50, and received a premium of $250. However, immediately prior to expiration, the stock's market value is only $44 per share. The value of the put is $600. The buyer could exercise the put, forcing you to buy 100 shares at $50 per share—$6 per share above current market value. You have two choices: First, let the buyer exercise the option, in the belief that $50 per share is a fair price. You then get to keep the $250 premium you received when you sold the put. Second, you could buy the put for $600, accepting a loss of $350. By buying the contract, the original position is canceled.

Selling options is a higher risk strategy than buying. Because options lose value as the expiration date approaches, you have an advantage as a seller: Time is on your side. But if the movement in the underlying stock is opposite what you expected, you stand to lose money. Sudden changes in the market value of stock can occur at any time, and the more volatility (see definition later in chapter) in the market and in the underlying stock, the greater are your risks as a seller.

A call seller's risks are unlimited, since a stock's value can rise indefinitely. The put seller's risk is finite—that is, limited to the difference between the contingent price of the stock and zero. A stock cannot fall below a zero value.

THE UNDERLYING STOCK

Option values change in direct relationship to the market value of the underlying stock. Every option is married to the stock of a specified company, and how the investor fares depends on how that stock's value changes in the future.

As shown in Table 1.1, you will consider price movement in the underlying security as a positive or as a negative, depending on whether you are a buyer or a seller and on whether you are involved with calls or puts.

Example: Two months ago, you bought a call, paying a premium of 3 points. (In the options market, "3" means the option's premium is $300.) The striking price was 40. At that time, the underlying

Table 1.1. Price Movement in the Underlying Security

	Increase in Price	Decrease in Price
Call buyer	Positive	Negative
Call seller	Negative	Positive
Put buyer	Negative	Positive
Put seller	Positive	Negative

stock's price was $40 per share. In this condition—when the option's premium is identical to the current price of the stock—the option is said to be *at the money*. Suppose the price of the stock increases so that it is above the option's striking price. In this case, a call is said to be *in the money*. And suppose the price of the stock decreases below the striking price. In this case, the call is said to be *out of the money*.

Figure 1.3 shows the in-, at-, and out-of-the-money ranges in comparison to a striking price of a call. For a put, the terms are reversed. When the current market value of the underlying stock is lower than the striking price of the put, it is in the money, and when that value is higher than the striking price of the put, it is out of the money.

The approximate dollar-for-dollar movement of an option occurs whenever an option is in the money. But when it is out of the money, changes in the value of the stock will not necessarily have an equal effect on the option premium.

Example: You bought a put last month with a striking price of $30 and paid 2 (a premium of $200). At the time, the stock's market price was $34 per share, or $4 out of the money. More recently, the stock's price fell to $31, a downward movement of

at the money: a condition in which the market value of the underlying security is identical to the striking price of the option

in the money: a condition in which the market value of the underlying stock is higher than the call's striking price or lower than the put's striking price

out of the money (the opposite of "in the money"): a condition in which the market value of the underlying stock is lower than the call's striking price or higher than the put's striking price

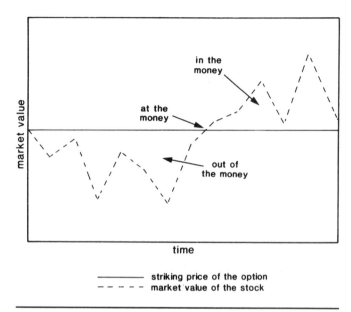

Figure 1.3.   Market value of the underlying stock.

3 points. However, your put has increased in value only 1½ points.The stock's market price continues to fall, going into the money (declining below the striking price of 30). Once in the money, the value of the option will move approximately dollar for dollar with changes in value of the underlying stock.

Example: You bought a call with a striking price of $45, and paid 3 ($300). At the time you bought the option, the stock's price was $44 per share. About two weeks later, the stock's price rose to $45 (at the money) but your option's value didn't change at all. However, when the stock then rose ½ point, the option also went up in value ½ point. The following week, the stock's price went up 7 points, and the option's premium value also rose 7 points. At that point, the call was worth $1050; you bought it for $300, it then went up in value $50, and then another $700. If you sold the option at that point, you would earn a profit of $750, less transaction fees. Note that when the option was in the money, price movements corresponded to price movements in the stock. But when it was out of the money, the option's premium value was not as sensitive.

The value of in-the-money options is inescapably related to movement in the price of the underlying stock. But "value" in the market also depends on two other factors. First is *volatility*—that is, the degree of change in the value of both the option and the underlying stock. Second is the time remaining from your transaction date until expiration. Changes in value are often anticipated or accompanied by changes in *volume*, the level of trading activity in a stock or option, or in the market as a whole. (The level of volume in an underlying stock will affect an option's premium.)

INTRINSIC VALUE AND TIME VALUE

A *listed option*'s premium consists of two parts. Its *intrinsic value* is that part represented by the degree that it is in the money. Any difference is *time value*, which declines over the life of the option so that, at the point of expiration, it is zero. The longer the time until that expiration date, the higher the time value premium.

Example: A call is available at a premium of 3 ($300) with a striking price of $45. At the time you buy the call, the underlying stock has a market value of $45 per share. In this instance, the entire value of the option's premium represents time value. The time value will decrease over the time

volatility: a measure of the degree of change in a stock's market price during a twelve-month period, stated as a percentage (To compute, you subtract the lowest price from the highest price during the twelve months and divide the difference by the annual low.)

volume: the level of trading activity in a stock, an option, or in the market as a whole

listed option: an option traded on a public exchange (Listed options are traded on the New York, Chicago, Pacific, American, and Philadelphia stock exchanges.)

intrinsic value: the amount the option is in the money (An at-the-money or out-of-the-money option has no intrinsic value.)

time value: the option's premium above any intrinsic value (When an option is at the money or out of the money, the entire premium represents time value.)

between now and expiration so that no time value will be left at the end. If the stock's price remains at or below the striking price, the entire premium value will be time value. For each dollar above striking price, there is an equal dollar of intrinsic value. So if the stock is at $46 at some point before expiration, the option will have intrinsic value of $1; any remaining value will be time value.

The comparison of option premium and the market value of the underlying stock in Table 1.2 reveals the direct relationships between intrinsic value, the market price of the underlying stock, and the declining nature of time value. Figure 1.4 shows how movement in the underlying stock is identical to the option's intrinsic value. When the stock is at the money or out of the money, there is

Table 1.2.   The Declining Time Value of an Option

Month	Stock Price	Option Premium (Striking Price of $45)		
		Total Value	Intrinsic Value[1]	Time Value[2]
1	$45	$3	$0	$3
2	47	5	2	3
3	46	4	1	3
4	46	3	1	2
5	47	4	2	2
6	44	2	0	2
7	46	2	1	1
8	45	1	0	1
9	46	1	1	0

[1] Intrinsic value reflects the price difference between the stock's current market value and the option's striking price.
[2] Time value is greatest when the expiration date is furthest away and declines as expiration approaches.

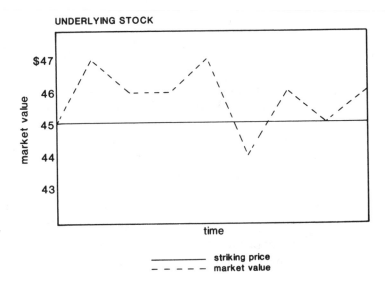

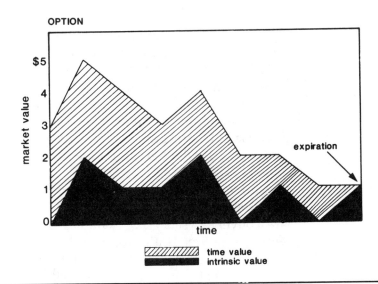

Figure 1.4.   Time and intrinsic values of underlying stock and options.

no intrinsic value. And when it is in the money, the intrinsic value matches the degree exactly. You can also see how time value depreciates over the life of the option.

The total amount of premium might vary between two different stocks at the same price due to perceptions of value. For example, two corporations have current options with striking prices of $55, and both are valued at $58 per share. But the option premium is 5 for one stock, and 7 for the other.

Time value for different stocks will not always change in an identical manner. The difference in perception among investors affects the total premium. For example, one company might be rumored as a takeover candidate. As a result, daily volume of trading in the stock is quite high, and the price of the stock is more volatile than other stocks of the same price. In that condition, the option's time value might also be higher. The *potential* for price movement in the stock, as well as perceptions among investors about the company, could create higher demand for both the stock and the related options. Call buyers are willing to pay more for the time value based on those perceptions. And because of the uncertainty, risks are greater for call sellers, and a higher premium is demanded for those risks.

Judging time value of an option is one important way to locate opportunities, whether you are a buyer or a seller. For example, suppose a stock with a long time until expiration has an unusually low time value. As a buyer, you recognize that the price for that option is represented primarily by intrinsic value, the tangible worth of the underlying stock. Or suppose a stock has an exceptionally high time value and a relatively short time until expiration. In this case, a seller receives a better than average premium and realizes that, as expiration approaches, the time value disappears rapidly.

You can easily recognize time value in an option premium by comparing the stock's current value and the option's price. For example, two stocks are currently priced at $47 per share. Options with striking prices of $45 are available for 3 on one stock and for 5 on the other.

Stock Price

Current market value	$47
Less striking price	45
Intrinsic value	$ 2

Option Premium

Option #1	$3
Less intrinsic value	2
Time value	$1

In the next chapter, striking price, expiration date, and exercise will be explained with regard to how they affect your option strategies.

CHAPTER 2

Opening, Closing, and Tracking the Option

terms: the complete description of an option, including the striking price, expiration month, type (call or put), and the underlying security

E very option is described by four attributes that are collectively called the *terms* of the option. These are the striking price, expiration month, type of option (call or put), and underlying stock.

In evaluating an option for risk and potential profits, the point of view of an option seller is different than that of the buyer. For each of the four terms of an option, what is an advantage to one is a disadvantage to the other.

1. *Striking price.* The striking price describes the fixed price of the underlying stock at which the option contract exists. As long as the option has not expired, the striking price is the set price to buy or sell 100 shares of stock. To the buyer, the striking price identifies the price at which you may buy 100 shares (for a call option) or sell 100 shares (for a put option), in the event you decide to exercise. For a seller, the striking price is the opposite. It identifies the price at which you may be required to sell 100 shares (for a call option) or buy 100 shares (for a put option), in the event the *buyer* exercises the option you sold.

2. *Expiration date.* Every option comes into being for only a limited number of months; that is the problem or the opportunity, depending on the strategies you employ. Every option must be canceled, exercised, or allowed to expire, but will not go on forever. This increases risks, since buyers might not be able to realize profits by the expiration date; it also increases opportunities, notably for sellers, since pending expiration decreases time value dramatically. Thus, for the seller, falling option premium value could represent profit, whereas for the buyer, expiration is more of a problem. For the seller, an option that has lost value and is out of the money will not be exercised.

3. *Type of option.* The distinction between calls and puts is extremely important; they are opposites of each other. So of course, the same strategies cannot be used for each option with the same results. The call gives the buyer the right to buy 100 shares, and the put gives the buyer the right to sell 100 shares. If you believe the underlying stock will increase in value, you would want to buy calls or sell puts; if you believe the stock's market price will fall, you would want to sell calls or buy puts. As you will see later, though, there are many reasons to buy or sell options, and many strategies possible, including the combined use of calls and puts at the same time.

4. *Underlying stock.* Every stock option is identified with a specific company's common stock. Only certain stocks have listed options available, and only on certain exchanges. Options cannot exist without the underlying stock, since it is the stock's market value that determines the option's premium as well as whether options are traded at all, and whether they will be exercised. All options available on one underlying stock are referred to as

class: all options traded on a single underlying security, including different striking prices and expiration dates

a single *class* of options. Thus, one stock might have a number of calls and puts with various striking prices and expiration dates. And all of those options with the same terms—striking price, expiration month, type (call or put), and underlying stock—are considered a single *series* of option.

series: a group of options sharing identical terms

A Note on the Expiration Cycle

Expiration for the options of a single underlying stock occurs within an expiration *cycle*. Every stock with listed options falls into one of these. The three cycles have expiration dates in:

cycle: the series of expiration dates on the options of a particular underlying stock (There are three cycles, according to expiration dates: (1) January, April, July, and October; (2) February, May, August, and November; and (3) March, June, September, and December.)

- January, April, July, and October
- February, May, August, and November
- March, June, September, and December

In addition to these fixed expiration cycle dates, active options might also be available for one-or two-month terms for the immediate future. For example, on issues with options expiring in the cycle month of April, there might also be contracts available on a short-term basis, so that in February, you can buy or sell options with expirations in March, April, July, or October.

The expiration of an option occurs on the third Saturday of the expiration month. An order for cancellation or exercise must occur on the *last trading day* prior to the indicated *expiration time* and day. If you are planning to take such an action at the last minute, be sure to find out, in advance, how and when you can take the action you want. You will probably need to place the sell order on Friday immediately before the Saturday expiration. You will lose the opportunity to sell if you don't act before the end of business on the preceding Friday.

last trading day: the Friday preceding the third Saturday of the expiration month of an option

Example: You purchased a July call and want to sell prior to expiration, which is the third Saturday in July. You must place your sell order by that date. You need to place your order on Friday, which is the last trading day for that option. Otherwise, the option would expire worthless and you would receive nothing.

OPENING AND CLOSING OPTION TRADES

Every option trade you make must specify all of the four terms: striking price, expiration month, call or put, and underlying stock. If any one of the terms changes, it becomes a different option.

Whenever you make a trade, the terms must be fully described. Later in this chapter, you will see how actual trades are done by way of a coded abbreviation involving symbols. For now, it is important to understand that there are two ways to open an option's position (buying and selling) and three ways to close an option's position (cancellation, exercise, or expiration).

Whenever you have bought an option and it has not yet closed, you are in an *open position*. If you buy an option to open a position, it is called an *opening purchase transaction*. And if you start out by selling an option, that is called an *opening sale transaction*.

Example: You purchased a call two months ago. When you purchased, it became an opening purchase transaction. That status remains so long as you don't take any further action, and so long as the call has not expired. The position is closed by sale, exercise, or expiration.

expiration time: the latest possible time to place an order for cancellation or exercise, which is 5:30 P.M. (New York time) on the Friday immediately preceding the third Saturday of the expiration month

open position: the status when a purchase (long) transaction or a sale (short) transaction has been made (The position remains open until cancellation, expiration, or exercise.)

opening purchase transaction: a transaction executed to buy, also known as "going long"

opening sale transaction: a transaction executed to sell, also known as "going short"

closed position:
the status of an
option that has
been canceled or
exercised or is
expired

**closing sale
transaction:** a sale
to close a previous
long position (For
example, if you
previously bought
an option, a
closing sale
transaction cancels
that position.)

**closing purchase
transaction:** a
purchase to close a
previous short
position (For
example, if you
previously sold an
option, a closing
purchase
transaction cancels
that position.)

Example: You sold a call last month, assuming a short position (the sale preceding the purchase). This was an opening sale transaction. If the option is held until expiration, it will become worthless and you will be able to realize a profit on the entire amount you received at sale. Another possible outcome is that the buyer on the other end will exercise the option, forcing you to buy 100 shares of the underlying stock, at the striking price. In that event, you also get to keep the entire amount of premium you received. The third possibility is that you will close the position by buying the option. The offsetting purchase cancels the open status of the option.

The actions or events that change an open position to a *closed position* are called closing transactions. When you are "long" (meaning you previously bought an option) and you sell the option, that is called a *closing sale transaction*. If you are "short" (meaning you previously sold an option) and you subsequently buy the option, that is called a *closing purchase transaction.*

All options are subject to a one-day settlement. That means that whenever you buy, you must make payment on the business day after the trade. If you sell, the proceeds are paid to your account on the next business day. In comparison, stock purchases and sales settle in five business days.

Example: You bought an option a number of months ago, for a premium of 2 ($200). Today, the same option is worth 5 ($500). You telephone your broker and instruct her to sell the option, thus realizing a profit of $300 before transaction fees. This trade is a closing sale transaction, since it cancels your ownership of the option. The proceeds are credited to your account on the following business day.

Example: You sold an option last month, assuming a short position. As long as that status remains unchanged, you are at risk of exercise. The buyer on the other end of the transaction can exercise at any time before expiration. You have the choice of waiting out the period until expiration, hoping to avoid going in the money (which would result in exercise). Or, you may choose to execute a closing purchase transaction. By offsetting the short position, you cancel the contract and the risk that goes with it.

DEFINING POSSIBLE OUTCOMES OF CLOSING OPTIONS

Every option will be canceled by an offsetting transaction, an exercise, or an expiration. The results of each are different for buyers and sellers.

Results for the Buyer

1. If you cancel your open position with a closing sale transaction, you receive payment. If the price is higher than your original purchase, you realize a profit; if lower, it's a loss.
2. If you exercise the option, you receive or sell 100 shares of the underlying stock at the striking price.
3. If you allow the option to expire, you lose the entire premium invested in the option.

Results for the Seller

1. If you cancel your open position with a closing purchase transaction, you must pay the premium on the following business day. If the price is lower than your original sale, you realize a profit; if higher, it's a loss. This outcome is opposite that for a buyer.

2. If the option is exercised, you must deliver 100 shares of the underlying stock at the striking price (if a call) or accept 100 shares at the striking price (if a put).

3. If the option expires worthless, you earn a profit. Your open position is canceled by the expiration, and the entire premium you received upon sale is yours to keep.

These outcomes are summarized in Figure 2.1. Notice that buyers and sellers have opposite results to a closed option. The buyer receives cash upon sale, while the seller pays. The buyer chooses to exercise the option, while the seller is on the passive side of that decision. And upon expiration, the buyer loses money, while the seller profits.

EXERCISING AN OPTION

Options transactions occur through the exchange on which the option is listed. While several differ-

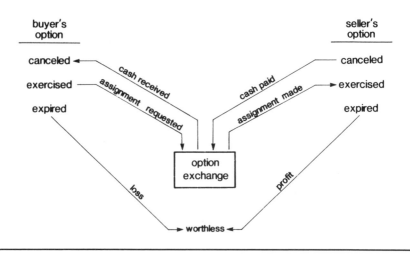

Figure 2.1.   Outcomes of closing the position.

ent exchanges handle trading of options, the Options Clearing Corporation (OCC) ensures the orderly settlement of all listed option contracts. When a seller notifies the OCC of the desire to exercise (through a broker and then through the listing exchange), the order is assigned to a buyer by the OCC. Notification is sent to a clearing member—a brokerage firm that handles its customers' accounts.

In this way, sellers do not have to rely directly on buyers to honor their obligations under the option contract. The OCC depends on clearing members to enforce *assignment*. Since there is no specific matching of open positions between buyers and sellers so long as options remain unexercised, the seller whose option is actually exercised is selected either on a random basis or on the basis of first-in, first-out (the earliest buyer will be the first one exercised). Upon exercise of the option, 100 shares must be delivered. *Delivery* is the physical movement of stock from one owner to another.

When a buyer decides to exercise, 100 shares of stock are either purchased (called from) or sold (put to) the buyer. The process of calling and putting stock upon exercise is called *conversion*. The stock is assigned at the time of exercise. When a call option is assigned, the stock is said to be *called away*.

Is exercise always a negative to the seller? The answer depends on his or her purpose in having taken a short position. Most option sellers prefer to avoid exercise by either closing the position or by selecting options they believe will be worthless by expiration date. Of course, a seller must also acknowledge that exercise can occur at any time. A buyer has the right to exercise the option far in advance of expiration date if he or she chooses to do so. This action is called *early exercise*.

In addition, *automatic exercise* is an action that

assignment: the act of exercise against a seller (When the buyer exercises an option, it is assigned to a seller, usually on a random basis.)

delivery: physical movement of stock from one owner to another (Shares are transferred upon registration of stock to the new owner and payment of the market value of those shares.)

conversion: the process of moving assigned stock from the seller of a call option or to the seller of a put option (Ownership is converted through the buyer's exercise of the option.)

called away: the result of having stock assigned (For each call option exercised, 100 shares of the seller's stock are called away at the striking price.)

early exercise: the act of exercising an option prior to expiration date (Buyers have the right to exercise at any time.)

automatic exercise: action taken by the Options Clearing Corporation at the time of expiration, when an in-the-money option has not been otherwise exercised or canceled.

can be taken by the OCC at an option's point of expiration. Remember that the options exchange acts as seller to every buyer and as buyer to every seller. It will match up exercise on the buyer's side against an open seller's position whenever possible. But if, at the time of expiration, there is an excess of sellers, in-the-money options will be exercised automatically.

The decision to avoid exercise is made on the basis of current market value. So long as the option is out of the money, there is no danger of exercise. Once the option goes in the money, the seller has to decide whether to take action to avoid exercise or to allow exercise to occur.

Example: You bought 100 shares of stock two months ago, paying $57 per share. You invested $5700 plus brokerage fees. Last month, the stock's market value was $62 per share. At that time, you decided to sell a call with a striking price of $60. As seller, you received a premium for that call of 7 ($700). You were willing to be placed in this short position. Your reasoning: If the call is exercised, your total profit will be $1000 before brokerage fees. That consists of 3 points per share (market value of $60, less your original cost of $57); plus $700 you were paid when you sold the call:

Striking price	$60
Less your cost per share	57
Stock profit	$ 3
Plus option premium	7
Total profit per share	$10

In this example, it's possible that you sold the in-the-money call, hoping for exercise. This is one way to sell your stock *and* receive additional income (from the option premium). At the same time, you protect profits already realized. In the event the price of the stock falls, you have received $700 for selling the option. So if the value of the underlying stock falls by 7 points, you have covered that loss.

Example: You sold a put recently, and were paid a premium of 3 ($300). The striking price was $35. At the time of your action, the stock was priced at $33 per share, and it is trading at approximately the same level now. Even though the option is $2 per share in the money, you are not concerned. If the put is exercised, you will have to buy 100 shares at $35 per share, or $2 per share higher than current market value. Three points should be made, however: First, the premium you received for the put was 3, more than covering the difference in market value and striking price. Second, when you sell a put, you should consider the striking price as a fair price for the stock, and should be willing to purchase it at that price. Third, if the stock's value rises above the striking price and remains there until expiration, it will not be exercised.

Example: You have owned 100 shares of stock for several years. You purchased the stock at $48 per share, but current market value is $59 per share. You want to sell a call against the stock. Recognizing that you are $11 per share ahead, you are willing to risk a part of that profit by selling a call. You decide to sell a call with a striking price of $55, or $4 in the money. For selling the call, you are paid a premium of 6 ($600). Even if you were paid only 4 ($400) for the call, you would lose nothing in the event of exercise. The sacrifice of market value would be equal to the premium paid for the call. In this case, you were paid 6, consisting of $4 for the in-the-money intrinsic value, plus $2 of time value.

**current market
value:** the market
value of stock at
the present time

The decision to act or wait often is determined by the amount of time value in the option premium. For the buyer, time value is generally a negative factor. You pay an amount above intrinsic value— the difference between *current market value* and striking price—knowing that the time value will disappear by the time of expiration. But as a seller, time value is potential profit. The greater the time value when you sell, the better is the chance for profit, because time value will disappear between now and expiration date.

Example: You have decided to speculate in options, and want to buy a call with a striking price of $30. The underlying stock is currently valued at $32 per share. The option's premium is 5 ($500). You will be paying $2 per share for intrinsic value (the difference between current market value and striking price), and $3 for time value. If the stock's market value does not increase by expiration, the time value will evaporate. The stock's market value must increase by 3 points in order for you to break even, and by more if you hope to profit.

Example: Now consider the same question from the seller's point of view: You plan to be the seller in this transaction instead of the buyer. The $300 time value is a benefit to you, not a problem. So long as the stock's market value does not increase by more than 3 points, selling this call will be profitable. The premium you were paid offsets any differences of 3 points or less between striking price and market value.

parity: the
condition of an
option when the
total premium is
identical to intrinsic
value and no time
value exists

By the point of expiration, all of the time value will have disappeared from the option's premium. At that point, the option is said to be at *parity*— that is, it consists entirely of intrinsic value.

Using the Daily Options Listings

Keeping in mind that expiration is constantly pending, both buyers and sellers of options must track their open positions. The opportunity for profit or the threat of loss can occur within a very short period of time.

An investor who buys stock can take a more leisurely approach. If you intend to hold that stock for many years, daily price movement will not be as critical to the value of your investment, and the consequences of missing an opportunity will not be as expensive.

You can estimate the value of your options by simply watching daily closing prices of the underlying stock.

Example: You purchased a call for 3 ($300), with a striking price of $50. Your goal is to sell when the stock's market price rises by 5 points or more. However, you also know that time is working against you. With this in mind, you want to anticipate the trends in the underlying stock. This is possible by tracking both the stock's price and the option's premium value on a daily basis. You can read the financial pages, which report the previous day's closing results; or you may use one of many automated systems to track stock market activity. If you do not have a computer system, you can call your broker for current stock and option information.

To select options to buy or sell or to track results in more detail, you will need to see daily option listings. *The Wall Street Journal* reports daily closing values of all listed options, and *Barron's* reports the same information weekly. Other local papers report option closing prices, but often in an abbreviated or partial format.

Figure 2.2 shows a typical daily option listing. The first column identifies the underlying stock and its current price. In this example, Delta Airlines closed at $37 per share. The second column reports the striking prices of all available options. As a general rule, stocks valued at $100 or less have options available at $5 striking price intervals; above $100, the usual interval is $10.

Columns three through five show current premiums for calls, and columns six through eight are put premiums. Delta Airlines has options on the January, April, July, and October cycle, so three different expiration dates are shown (options only exist for nine months, so the month in the cycle that is furthest away will not be shown; in this example, the October column will appear only after the January options have expired). Notice that the options with the greatest amount of time until expiration have higher time values than those that will expire sooner.

In this example, Delta's current market value is $37 per share. So the $35 calls are $2 in the money. The January contracts reflect time value of only ⅝ of a point. Time value in the longer term options is greater. And the $30 option has 7 points of time

		CALLS			PUTS		
		JAN	APR	JUL	JAN	APR	JUL
Delta	25	12	14	17 ½	¹⁄₁₆	s	s
37	30	7 ½	8 ⅜	9	r	⅛	r
37	35	2 ⅝	5 ⅛	7	⅜	2	3 ½
37	40	⅛	1 ½	r	3 ¼	5	r
37	45	r	r	s	8 ½	11	14 ⅛

r – no trades this date
s – not offered

Figure 2.2.   Example of daily option listing.

value. On the put side, the $40 contract is $3 in the money, and current premium values reflect intrinsic value of at least that much.

Making an Evaluation

An option buyer's evaluation of an option's listing will involve judgments about:

- Recent volatility and volume in the underlying stock.
- Time until expiration of specific option contracts.
- The amount of intrinsic and time value.
- Current premium levels.

Example: You are interested in buying calls on a particular stock you have been following. You recognize that certain stocks experience price movements desirable for particular option strategies. The stock is presently selling for $47 per share. You eliminate calls with striking prices of $35 and $40 as being too expensive. And the $55 striking price is 8 full points out of the money. Considering the problems of time value, the most likely purchase prospects for you are those calls with $45 or $50 striking prices. Remember, though, that the considerations for option sellers are completely different and, in some cases, opposite.

In this example, the $45 option is 2 points in the money, so you know that the value of the option will change almost dollar for dollar with the underlying stock. If the stock rises by $2 per share, the $45 calls will increase in value by 2 ($200). But if the stock falls to $45 per share, the option will also lose by the same amount.

The January option will expire very soon. If you

buy that option, you are paying for very little time value, and from that point of view alone, it is the best bargain for your money. However, with a short expiration, you also take the risk that the option will expire before the stock increases in value. These are offsetting points: low time value versus a short time until expiration. If you buy the option now and the stock goes up 1 point, you could make a profit of $100. The change in value could occur within a single day. But you could also lose the entire investment if the stock does not increase in value.

You must also consider the commission cost in an option transaction. If you buy or sell single-option contracts, the typical commission will be $30 to $35, charged both when you buy and when you sell. Thus a rise of 1 point could net you only $30 after commissions are taken out.

The process of elimination and risk appraisal can also be applied to puts. In order to profit from buying puts, you must depend on a decline in the stock's value before expiration—to a degree sufficient to:

- Offset time value premium.
- Cover the commission costs of buying and selling.
- Yield a reasonable profit.

If you sell an option, higher time value is a benefit rather than a disadvantage. But a longer time period until expiration increases your risks.

Understanding Option Abbreviations

Option values are expressed in daily option listings in abbreviated form. The value of a contract is always expressed in value per 100 shares. As shown in Table 2.1, 3 means $300, and 2⅝ means $262.50. Options trade down to fractional values as small as sixteenths of a point, with each sixteenth being equal to $6.25.

The abbreviated expression of options and their terms go beyond the current premium. Both the expiration month and the striking price are expressed in a shortened version as well. For example, an October option with a striking price of $35 per share is called an OCT 35 option. And a January option with a $50 striking price is a JAN 50. Like the premium value, the striking price is expressed without dollar signs.

A complete option description is shown in Figure 2.3. In this example, all of the terms, plus the current premium, are shown. Collectively, the terms distinguish a particular option from all other options.

When you call a broker to make an option trade, you can give directions without using abbreviations. But the broker must translate your instructions to place the order, which could result in an error. Brokers and option customers use a series of

Table 2.1. Fractional Values

Fraction	Dollar Value	Fraction	Dollar Value
¹⁄₁₆	$ 6.25	⁹⁄₁₆	$ 56.25
⅛	12.50	⅝	62.50
³⁄₁₆	18.75	¹¹⁄₁₆	68.75
¼	25.00	¾	75.00
⁵⁄₁₆	31.25	¹³⁄₁₆	81.25
⅜	37.50	⅞	87.50
⁷⁄₁₆	43.75	¹⁵⁄₁₆	93.75
½	50.00	1	100.00

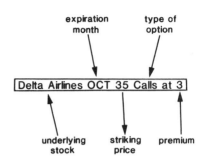

Figure 2.3. A complete option description.

symbols to identify the expiration month and the striking price. Figure 2.4 summarizes the symbols that are used by virtually all brokerage firms that trade options for their customers.

The expiration month is always given first, followed immediately by the striking price. Note that the symbol for striking prices of 5, 105, and 205 are identical. One symbol is used for all three, since the daily price of the underlying stock dictates which of the three prices applies.

An example of a specific option: You want to trade in call options with October expiration and a $35 striking price. The symbol (from Figure 2.4) consists of "J" for the expiration month and "G" for the striking price. Thus, this is a JG option. If the option were a put, the symbol would be VG instead of JG.

The option quote also includes an abbreviated symbol for the underlying stock. Every listed stock has its own unique code. Delta Airlines, for example, is described as DAL. So a Delta Airlines call with a striking price of $35 per share, expiring next October, consists of five digits. As illustrated in Figure 2.5, the stock code is listed first, followed by

expiration month symbols		
MONTH	CALLS	PUTS
January	A	M
February	B	N
March	C	O
April	D	P
May	E	Q
June	F	R
July	G	S
August	H	T
September	I	U
October	J	V
November	K	W
December	L	X

striking price symbols			
STRIKING PRICE			SYMBOL
5	105	205	A
10	110	210	B
15	115	215	C
20	120	220	D
25	125	225	E
30	130	230	F
35	135	235	G
40	140	240	H
45	145	245	I
50	150	250	J
55	155	255	K
60	160	260	L
65	165	265	M
70	170	270	N
75	175	275	O
80	180	280	P
85	185	285	Q
90	190	290	R
95	195	295	S
100	200	300	T
7½	–	–	U
12½	–	–	V
17½	–	–	W
22½	–	–	X

Figure 2.4.   Option trading symbols.

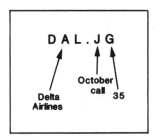

Figure 2.5.   Example of option quote.

a period and the two-letter code identifying the month and the striking price.

SETTING STANDARDS

Before entering any option trade, you need to establish specific standards for yourself. Of course, this is true for all types of investing; otherwise, you cannot know when to make decisions, because you have not decided what you need and want. Several questions come up with option transactions, such as:

- Should the position be closed or allowed to expire?
- On what basis should the decision to close be made? Should you establish a minimum profit that you can accept, or a maximum loss that you can tolerate?
- What types of options should you buy, and for what purpose?
- How much money should you invest and keep at risk?
- What portion of your portfolio or available cash should be placed into options?

Setting standards helps you to decide what level of risk is acceptable and appropriate. This is necessary at every phase of investing. Without the standard, you cannot measure how successfully you are executing your plan—because there isn't yet a plan. Identification of risk is crucial to success in the market, and particularly in the options market.

Example: You purchase a call and pay 3 ($300). The option will expire in seven months. In this case, you are accepting the risk that the underlying stock's market value will not go in the money sufficiently to yield a profit higher than $300 (your cost). No matter where that market value sat at the time of your purchase, it must be high enough to yield you this profit at some time prior to expiration. That usually means it will have to be in the money at least that much at some point during the next seven months. So by buying the call, you were willing to risk losing $300 in exchange for the potential gain. An example of setting a standard would be to decide you will sell the call if it gains enough to make the premium 5 ($500) or more. You will be wise to understand the risk *and* to set a standard before embarking on any strategy.

Example: You have 100 shares of stock in your portfolio, currently valued at $46 per share. You sell a call with a striking price of $45 and receive a premium of 4 ($400). You know that if this call is exercised, your stock will be called away at $45 per share. The risk is that the stock's market value will increase substantially above this level. However, you are willing to accept that risk in exchange for the certainty of receiving $400 for the premium today. You have set a standard for yourself. It states: You are willing to let the stock go for $45 per share in exchange for $400. You are willing to have the option exercised even if the stock is worth much more. You can set additional standards as well. For example, you may decide that if the option's value declines by two points, you will buy and close the position, accepting a $200 profit and canceling the remaining stock risk.

What happens if you don't set a standard? You might fall into a pattern in which you can never win. This is the typical experience of people who should not trade options, because they are unable to resist current trends. Rather than operating from a firm standard, they react to what appears to be happening from day to day.

Example: You bought a put two weeks ago, in the belief that the underlying stock's market value would fall. You paid a premium of 2 ($200). You originally hoped to double your money, meaning the stock would have to fall 2 points or more. The put would then increase in value dollar for dollar once in the money. As of last week, the stock's market value had fallen 3 points and your put option is worth 5 ($500). You could have sold then and realized a profit of $300. But you did not sell, because you thought the stock might continue its downward movement. You called your broker three days ago, only to discover that the stock had rebounded 2 points. Your option was then worth 3 ($300). You realized you should have sold when you had the chance. So you resolved to sell if the stock fell again, and if your put's value rose to $500.

Yesterday, the stock's value fell to its lowest point yet, down 4 points. The put was worth 7 ($700). You knew you should sell, but again you wondered if there would be more profit for waiting. So you waited. Today, the stock rebounded again by several points, and your put is now worth only $100.

This type of indecision is not uncommon. Many paper profits have been lost because investors had not set standards; or if they had standards, they were unable to live with them when the decision point arrived. You are better off losing future profit potential than you are losing actual profits today. If you are willing to take greater risks and pass up short-term profits, you also need to be willing to have more losses than the speculator who sets and follows specific rules.

You can set and enforce your own standards with the use of stop orders, which are contingent orders you can place with your broker.

Example: You purchased a call last week for 6 ($600), also placing a stop order for 4. If the option's value falls to 4 or below, a sale will be automatically executed as soon as possible. This does *not* mean you will get $400. If the price is falling rapidly, the premium value could be lower than 4 at the time the sell order is actually executed.

Example: You buy a call for 4 ($400) and place a stop order for 3. If the value falls to 3 or below, a sale will be executed automatically as soon as possible. There is no guarantee that the order will go through at 3. The trade will be executed as soon as possible, but if the price is falling rapidly, the actual sale price could be well below your target price.

A stop-limit order is more specific and limits losses. Using the same example, a stop-limit order tells the floor broker that the transaction must occur at that price. So if the option is worth 3, it will be executed, but if the option has already fallen below that level, the stop-limit order prevents the sale.

Stop orders can be entered for either buy or sell transactions and can be very useful in enforcing your standards—both for taking profits and for limiting losses.

A word of caution: Not all exchanges allow the use of stop orders for option trading. Before deciding to employ the stop order as part of your strategy, check with your broker and make sure that stop orders are allowed.

Many investors have experimented in the options market and have failed. Why? Because they did not appreciate the absolute necessity for setting a standard and sticking with it.

CALCULATING RATE OF RETURN FOR SELLERS

When you sell options, the rate of return you can expect depends on whether the following conditions apply:

1. You own 100 shares of the underlying stock for each option you sell.
2. The option is exercised.
3. You close the position after favorable decline in premium value.
4. The stock price changes significantly.

The rate of return should always be compared on an annualized basis. If you make a 12 percent profit in two investments, but you hold one for three months and the other for two years, the annual return is substantially different. To annualize a rate of return, you divide the percentage by the number of months held and then multiply the result by 12. For example, the annual return on a 12 percent profit earned in three months is

$$12\% \div 3 = 4.00\%$$
$$4.00\% \times 12 = 48.00\% \text{ annual return}$$

The annual return on 12 percent profit earned in two years is

$$12\% \div 24 = 0.50\%$$
$$0.50\% \times 12 = 6.00\% \text{ annual return}$$

To evaluate the potential return from selling an option, there are two comparative estimates of the rate of return: if exercised and if unchanged.

Return if exercised is what you will earn if the underlying stock will be called away. *Return if unchanged* is what you will earn if the option is not exercised. Total income from all sources (gain on the stock, if any, plus dividends and call premium) is divided by the original investment to compute the actual return.

In computing actual return, you must allow for the commissions paid at purchase and at sale. The amount of commission varies by broker and also depends on the number of options involved in a single trade. The more contracts, the lower is the rate of commission.

return if exercised: the estimated rate of return an option seller will earn in the event of exercise (The calculation includes profit on the purchase and sale of the underlying stock, dividends, and premium received.)

Example: You have 100 shares of stock in your portfolio that you originally purchased for $58 per share. The stock's current market value is $63 per share. You sell a call with a striking price of $60, receiving a premium of 7 ($700). Between the time of selling and expiration, you are paid two dividends, totaling $68:

return if unchanged: the estimated rate of return an option seller will earn if the option is not exercised (The assumption is that the stock will remain out of the money until expiration, so that the return will consist of the call premium and any dividends earned on the underlying stock.)

Return if Exercised

Striking price	$6000
Original cost	5800
Profit	$ 200
Plus dividends	68
Plus call premium	700
Total profit	$ 968
Return if exercised ($968/$5800)	16.69%

Return if Unchanged

Call premium	$ 700
Plus dividends	68
Total profit	$ 768
Return if unchanged ($768/$3800)	13.24%

The next step is to annualize the return. For example, if the time between your purchase of the stock and expiration of the option is nine months, the return if exercised is

$$16.96\%/9 = 1.85\%$$
$$1.85\% \times 12 = 22.20\%$$

and the return if unchanged is

$$13.24\%/9 = 1.47\%$$
$$1.47\% \times 12 = 17.64\%$$

One problem in comparing these calculations is that the first (return if exercised) is based on the idea that the underlying stock is actually sold. That means you no longer own the stock, will have a capital gain on which to pay taxes, and have a large sum of cash to reinvest. The second (return if unchanged) assumes that you profit based on your basis in the stock, but you still own the stock after expiration. Obviously, these outcomes are far from comparative.

However, consider the way that these computations can be used. In deciding whether to enter a particular option transaction, an understanding of the possible outcomes—exercise or unchanged—can help you to judge risks and potential profits. With this in mind, the relatively easy calculations are valuable to you in entering an option transaction.

In computing the return if exercised, the calculation involves an offsetting profit and loss if the striking price of the option is lower than the original price level you paid for the underlying stock.

Example: You bought 100 shares of stock last year and paid $37 per share. Last month, you sold a call with a striking price of $35 ($2 below your basis price). You are paid a premium of 6; you also will receive $40 in dividends between now and the expiration date.

Return if Exercised

Striking price	$ 3500
Original cost	3700
Loss	$ (200)
Plus dividends	40
Plus call premium	600
Net profit	$ 440
Return if exercised ($440/$3700)	11.89%

As an aware options trader, you must calculate the risks in advance of making a trade and set standards you will follow. These standards identify the desired level of profit you hope to achieve and also limit the amount of loss you are willing to accept. Any options investor who experiences an unexpected loss has simply failed to evaluate the ramifications of a particular trade.

Success in the options market means entering an open position with complete awareness of what can happen. You must know when you will cancel a position with an offsetting closing transaction, when to exercise or what will happen if your option is exercised, and what happens upon expiration. You should always have complete knowledge about an investment before you make a decision. But knowledge of profit potential is not enough. You must also be fully aware of the risks that are involved.

CHAPTER 3

Buying Calls

A call grants the buyer the right to buy 100 shares of a specific stock. The premium paid to acquire the call gives you that right. And as a call owner, you have a choice to make in the future. You may sell the call before it expires; you may exercise the call and buy 100 shares; or you may let the call expire worthless.

You are never obligated to buy 100 shares if you are the buyer. The seller, in contrast, would have to buy 100 shares if the buyer exercised the option. The decision you make as owner of a call will depend on:

- The actual movement of the underlying stock and the resulting effect on the call's value.
- Your reasons for buying the call in the first place.
- Your risk posture and willingness to wait out the future movement of the stock and the option, versus taking a sure-thing profit today.

UNDERSTANDING THE LIMITED LIFE OF THE CALL

You can become a call buyer purely in the interest of making a profit within a limited amount of time. That profit can be made by selling the call at a higher price than you paid for it or by exercising to buy stock below the market value or to offset losses in a short position in the underlying stock. These uses of calls are explained later in this chapter.

You must understand your risks as a buyer before entering this market. Since the calls you purchase will exist for only a limited number of months, you must achieve your purpose as an investor before expiration. Otherwise, you stand to lose the entire premium.

Anyone who has purchased shares of stock knows that time is a luxury. You can hold onto your shares for a day, a week, or for many years. The decision is yours when to sell. Many people buy shares of stock for future appreciation or regular dividend payments over time. Call buyers do not enjoy these privileges. For them, time is not a luxury.

A simple comparison between investing in stock and purchasing a call option puts call options strictly in the arena of *speculation*. Because they are rights and not tangible properties and because their existence is limited by time, the call is nothing more than a side bet. A buyer bets that the market will rise, while a seller bets that the market will fall. Fast—and significant—profits or losses can and do occur for call buyers, and knowing the extent of those profits or losses is an important first step.

To judge the *suitability* of investing in calls, you must comprehend the risks involved and be able to afford taking those chances. You should always know the risks of any investment before making it and be financially able to stand the losses that might occur.

Example: One investor has no experience whatsoever in the market. He has never owned stock before and does not know how the market works. He

speculation: a risky use of money to create immediate or short-term profits, with the knowledge that substantial or total losses are also likely (Buying calls for leverage is a form of speculation: The buyer might earn a large profit in a short period of time or lose the entire premium.)

suitability: a standard by which an investment or market strategy is judged (The investor's knowledge and experience in options is an important suitability standard, and a strategy is appropriate only if the investor can afford the risks that are involved.)

has $1000 available to invest today, and decides he wants to make a profit as fast as possible. A friend told him about the kinds of profits available by buying calls. He needs the money by September, when a debt will be payable. Even though he cannot afford to lose the $1000, he buys three calls for 3 ($300) each. If the stock goes up 3 points, he will double his money; if the stock doesn't move at all or if it goes down, he will lose the entire investment.

Buying calls is not a suitable investment in this case. The investor cannot afford the losses, and only one possibility has been considered: what happens if the value of the underlying stock goes up. If he is wrong, he stands to lose the entire $1000. The underlying stock might be a solid, secure company with great future potential. But the call buyer depends strictly on timing. If the purchase is made at the wrong time, those profits will not be realized by expiration date.

Example: An investor has several years of experience in the stock market. Even though she has never played the options market, she has been reading about it recently and has started tracking a few options in the daily financial pages. She has the majority of her portfolio in relatively secure and well-diversified stocks and mutual funds. She also has a sum of $1000 she is willing to risk in the options market. She decides to purchase three calls for 3 ($300) each, knowing full well the extent of risk.

So long as this individual understands the risks of buying a call, it can be a suitable way to speculate. If she knows that time works against the call buyer and that timing of the purchase can make the difference between profit and loss, she will be making an informed decision. She is also prepared for the loss and can afford it.

Suitability in the options market refers both to your ability to take losses and to your knowledge about the risks of this market.

JUDGING THE CALL

Most call buyers lose money. Even when the underlying stock does increase in value, that increase is often not substantial enough to offset the decline in time value.

Example: You recently bought a call at 4 ($400) when it was at the money. The striking price was $45 and the stock was at $45 per share at the time you made your decision. By expiration, the stock had risen to $47, but the call was worth only 2 ($200). Why? The entire $400 investment was time value, which disappeared by expiration. All the remaining value was intrinsic. The best action just before expiration would be to sell and accept the loss of $200; the alternative is to lose the entire investment by allowing the call to expire.

Example: You purchased a call two months ago at ⅜ ($37.50) when the stock was 7 points below the striking price. Now expiration is a day away. The stock has experienced a dramatic rise of 6 points. The option, though, is nearly worthless. The entire value was time value, and at the point of expiration—even with a significant rise in out-of-the-money value—there is no intrinsic value available.

Call buyers will lose money if they fail to set goals for themselves: If the premium value falls below their original cost, they do not close the position, hoping to recapture their original cost before expiration; if the value of the stock rises, they hesitate, hoping for yet more profits before expiration. The successful call buyer sets limits and goals and lives by them.

Example: You are the type of investor who believes in setting specific rules. So when you purchased a call at 4 ($400), you promised yourself you would sell on the downside if the option's value fell to 2 ($200) and accept a $200 loss. You also vowed to sell if its value rose to 7 ($700), in which case you would have a $300 profit. You reasoned that if you followed your own rules, you would limit your losses and take your profits when available. You know that with options, time is always limited. And, as an option buyer, you might not get a second chance.

realized profits or losses: profits or losses that are taken when an investor closes a position

Realized profits occur only if profits that can be earned are taken. You must decide at what point you will sell before actually buying a call, and you must stick to that rule. Otherwise, you will earn *paper profits* but end up with actual losses.

paper profits or losses (also called unrealized profits or losses): values that exist only because the current market value is higher or lower than the investor's basis (These profits or losses can be realized—taken—only by closing the position.)

Most call buyers study four attributes: current premium value, the portion of that premium that represents time value, months until expiration, and their own perception of the company. For example, you might look through the listings in *The Wall Street Journal*, seeking a call that is available for a premium of 2 or less, that is at the money or close to it, that has at least three months until expiration, and that is available on a company you consider a strong prospect for growth. This method is flawed. The smallest premiums do not necessarily equal the greatest values.

The best premium values for options with the longest time until expiration are those that are the greatest number of points out of the money. If the striking price is 40, and the stock is now worth less than $35 per share, you can probably buy a call with six months until expiration for a very low price. Of course, you also need that stock to increase enough in value so that the option will have intrinsic value greater than your cost at the point of expiration. Or the total premium must be greater than your cost at some point before expiration.

Example: You purchased a call with a striking price of $40 and paid a premium of 1 ($100). The option will expire in seven months, meaning there is a lot of time for the stock's market price to change. The stock is now at $34 per share, or 6 points out of the money. In order for you to realize a profit on this call, the stock must be selling above $41 per share by expiration (intrinsic value is equal to all in-the-money points); or it must appreciate in value enough before expiration date so that the call's premium value is greater than $100, meaning short-term appreciation.

Profits are possible in this situation without the stock's value even going in the money. If the stock increases several points shortly after you purchase the call, the premium value might go up 1 or 2 points. You can then sell the call and take a profit.

The more out of the money, the lower is the cost of the call—and the greater the risk that you will never realize a profit. As shown in Figure 3.1, whenever the stock is more than 5 points below the striking price, it is said to be *deep out* of the money. And if the stock is more than 5 points above the striking price, it is *deep in* the money.

deep in/deep out: terms describing an option when the underlying stock is more than 5 points above or 5 points below the striking price

ESTABLISHING GOALS

Most people think of buying options as a purely speculative activity. If the price goes up, you make

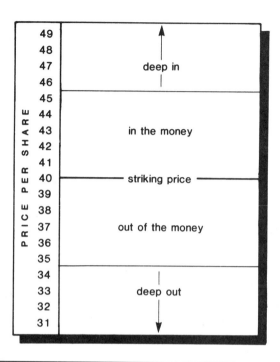

Figure 3.1.   Deep in/deep out stock prices.

a profit, and if it goes down, you lose. While that is a basic fact about the speculative nature of simply buying calls to make a profit, they can also be used for more conservative reasons.

leverage: the use of a limited amount of money to control greater values (A call buyer who spends $300 to control $5000 worth of stock has more leverage than an investor who spends $5000 to buy 100 shares.)

Goal 1: Gaining Leverage

Leverage is the most common reason for buying calls—that is, they create the potential for substantial gain with a limited amount of money. To show how quickly such profits (or losses) can occur, let's assume that you are comparing risks between the purchase of 100 shares of stock and a call that will expire in four months. See Figure 3.2.

	STOCK (1)		CALL (2)	
	PROFIT OR LOSS	RATE OF RETURN	PROFIT OR LOSS	RATE OF RETURN
price increase of 5 points	$500	8.1%	$500	100%
price increase of 1 point	$100	1.6%	$100	20%
no price change	0	0	0	0
price decrease of 1 point	-$100	-1.6%	-$100	-20%
price decrease of 5 points	-$500	-8.1%	-$500	-100%

(1) purchased at $62 per share ($6200)

(2) striking price 60, premium 5 ($500)

Figure 3.2.   Rate of return: buying stocks versus calls.

The stock is selling at $62 per share. You may either buy 100 shares, which will cost $6200, or you can purchase a call with a striking price of 60 for a more limited investment of 5 ($500). Of the total premium, 2 points represent intrinsic value and 3 points are time value.

If you buy 100 shares of the stock, you must pay for your purchase within five business days. If you buy a call, you must make payment on the business day following the transaction. These payment deadlines are the *settlement dates*.

As a call buyer, your plan is to sell the option before expiration. Like most call buyers, you have no intention of exercising the option, but are hop-

settlement date: the date on which an investor must pay for purchases or is paid for sales (Stock settlement occurs five business days after the transaction date; option settlement occurs on the business day following the transaction.)

ing for enough of an increase in value to make a profit before expiration.

For $500, you have control over 100 shares of stock. That's leverage. You do not need to invest $6200 to have that control. Without considering the commission cost of buying and selling the option, what could happen in the immediate future?

If the stock rises 5 points, the stockholder's $500 profit represents an 8.1% return, but the call buyer will realize a 100% return: the 5 points of profit on a $500 investment. The profit will occur only if the increase in the call's value occurs rather quickly. The longer it takes for this profit to occur, the more deterioration will occur from reduced time value. If the stock has increased at the point of expiration to $67 per share, the option will be worth 7 rather than 10, and the 3 points of time value will be gone.

An increase of 1 point in value yields 1.6% to the stockholder, but 20% to the option buyer. If there is no price change, you will be able to sell your call for the same price you paid (less commissions)—again, assuming you sell the option *before* time value declines. If you wait too long, the premium will diminish between purchase and expiration dates. For example, if the stock stays at $62 per share, your option (originally costing you 5) will decline in value to 2 at the expiration date.

As a call buyer, you are under the pressure of time for two reasons. First, the option will expire at a specified date in the future. And second, as you approach expiration, time value declines. This is why the chances of loss are high for buyers. An increase in value of the underlying stock is not enough. That increase must yield a profit above and beyond the time value in the premium you pay.

You can buy calls that have little or no time

value. But to do so, you must select calls that are close to expiration, which means you have only a short time for the stock to increase in value.

Example: In the second week of May, the May 50 call on an underlying stock is selling for 2, and the stock is worth 51⅝ (1⅝ points in the money). You buy one call. By the third Friday (next week), you hope for an increase in the underlying stock's value. If the stock goes up by 1 point, the option will be profitable.

Because time is short, your chances of realizing a profit are limited. But profits—if they do occur—will be close to dollar for dollar with movement in the stock. If that stock jumps 3 points, you could double your money in a few days. If it declines by 2 points, you will lose all or most of your premium.

The more time until expiration, the greater is the time value premium—and the more increase you need in the underlying stock just to maintain value. See Figure 3.3.

Example: You buy an option for 5 when the stock is at or near the striking price. The advantage is that you have eight months until expiration. The underlying stock remains fairly close to the striking price until the last two months, when it moves up to $33 per share. But because all of the time value has disappeared, your option is only worth 3, and you have lost $200.

Buying calls for leverage (controlling 100 shares of stock for a small amount of money) offers the potential for substantial gain. But because of time value and the ever-pending expiration, the risks are also great. Even with the best timing and analy-

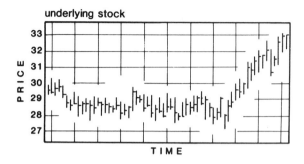

underlying stock

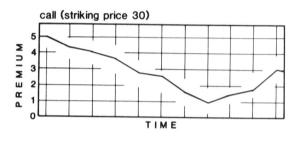

call (striking price 30)

Figure 3.3.   Diminishing time value of the call relative to the underlying stock.

sis, it is extremely difficult to consistently earn profits by buying calls and hoping for timely price increases.

Goal 2: Limiting Risks

In one respect, the limited amount of money you put into buying a call *reduces* your risks. A stockholder's losses are greater when a stock falls many points.

Example: You purchased a call two months ago for a premium of 5 ($500). It is scheduled to expire this month and is virtually worthless, since the

stock's market price has fallen 12 points—well below the striking price. You have lost the entire $500
but, in comparison, stockholders have lost $1200
for every 100 shares owned. You controlled as
much stock with less capital at risk. And, when the
loss did occur, your loss was smaller. In comparison, the stockholders enjoy the luxury of time.
They can hold onto their shares indefinitely, hoping the price will rebound. For the moment, however, the value of their investment is lower than
market value a few months before.

The time factor impedes the value of limiting
risks. You benefit only so long as the option exists,
with expiration a reality you cannot escape. The
stockholder has more money at stake, but is not
concerned with expiration dates.

It would make no sense to buy calls *only* to limit
risks. That's a side benefit to leverage. You must
assume that if you buy a call, it is in the expectation
of rising stock prices in the immediate future. But
in the event you are wrong, your losses are limited
to the amount you risk in premium.

Goal 3: Planning Future Purchases

When you own a call, you fix the price of a future
purchase in the event you do decide to exercise.
This use of calls goes beyond pure speculation.

Example: The market recently experienced a severe drop in value. You have been following the
stock of one company, which previously was trading in a range between $50 and $60 per share. After
the drop, that stock is valued at $39. You would
like to buy 100 shares at today's depressed value.
Your belief is that when the market does turn
around, the stock will prove to be a bargain at its

current price, but you do not have the $3900 to buy 100 shares. You will receive enough cash to make your purchase in about six months, but you don't want to miss the opportunity to buy 100 shares now.

To fix the price, you can buy a call while market values are low, with the intention of exercising that call when you do have the money. The 40 call is selling for 3, and you purchase one contract at that price. Six months later, the stock has increased to $58 per share. The option is worth 18 just before its expiration date.

You have a choice. You can either sell your call for 18, realizing a profit of $1500 (18 less your cost of 3). Or you can exercise the call and buy 100 shares at $40 per share. If you are seeking long-term growth and prefer the permanent value of owning stock, this is one way to use options—that is, to buy a call when you consider stock prices a bargain and, later, to exercise a purchase of stock at below-market prices.

If you were wrong and the value of the stock does not increase, you lose the premium you invested. But you also avoid the risk of buying stock that did not increase in value as you had expected.

Goal 4: Insuring Profits

A final reason to buy calls is to protect a short position in the underlying stock. Most investors buy stocks, hoping values will rise in the future. At some point, they mean to sell those shares and realize a profit. Other investors believe values will fall, and they sell shares, taking a short position. If they are right, values will decline, and their short positions can be closed out at a profit.

Example: An investor sells short 100 shares when market value is $58 per share. A month later, the stock's value has fallen to $52. He makes a closing purchase transaction—buying 100 shares—and realizes a profit of $600.

A short seller's risks are virtually unlimited. If he is wrong and values increase, he can close a position only by buying 100 shares at a higher price than the market value at the time the short sale was made. To protect themselves against this risk, short sellers often buy calls.

Example: An investor sells short 100 shares when market value is $58 per share. At the same time, she buys one call with a striking price of $65 for a premium of $\frac{7}{8}$ ($87.50). Her risk is no longer unlimited. If market value rises above $65 per share, the value of the call protects the position. Risk is limited to 7 points (between her short sale price of $58 and the call's striking price of $65).

In this case, a deep-out-of-the-money call is fairly inexpensive, yet it provides a form of insurance to the short seller. Of course, this protection is good only as long as the call exists. So the short seller must either decide to exercise the call before expiration or replace it with another call before expiration.

The short seller reduces and limits risk, but also reduces the likely profit by buying calls. The premium paid for that protection can be expensive if the value of calls is too high.

Example: A short seller must pay a premium of 2 for the call he needs over the next eight months. If the value of the stock declines by 2 points, he would normally be able to realize a $200 profit. But because he also paid for insurance in the form of a call, he will have only broken even at that point.

Profit in the short sale	$ 200
Loss in the call purchase	(200)
Profit	$ 0

Calls serve an important function when used by short sellers to limit risks. But they also take part of the profit away from the short selling strategy. In the event the stock does fall in value, the short seller will absorb the premium cost. But if stock values do climb, having the protection of the call can save thousands of dollars.

DEFINING PROFIT ZONES

Whatever strategy you employ in your portfolio, you should always be aware of what is required to create a profit and to what ranges of potential loss you expose yourself. You need to know the *break-even price* of your investment, as well as the *profit* and *loss zones*. See Figure 3.4.

break-even price (also called break-even point): the price of the underlying stock at which the option investor breaks even (For the call buyer, this price amounts to the number of points above the striking price of the stock that equals the price of the call before allowing for commission costs.)

profit zone: the price range of the underlying stock in which the option investor will realize a profit (For a call buyer, the profit zone extends upward from the break-even price.)

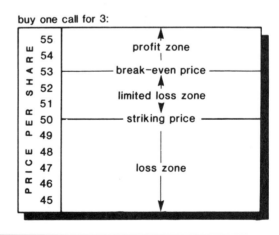

Figure 3.4.   A call's profit and loss zone.

Example: You buy a call at a premium of 3, with a striking price of 50. What must the stock's price be by the point of expiration to break even? What price must the stock achieve to create a profit? And at what price will you suffer a loss?

A loss occurs if the option expires out of the money (below the striking price). Because you paid a premium of 3, when the price is 3 points or less above striking price, you will suffer a limited loss. That is, if at the point of expiration the stock is worth $52 per share, you can sell your call for 2 and take a loss of $100. If the stock's value is at $53 per share, you are at the break-even point (without considering commission costs). And if the stock's price is above that level, you are in the profit zone.

Defining profit and loss zones and the break-even price helps you develop a goal for yourself when considering a call purchase. You must be willing to limit losses when stock values decline rather than rise and to take profits when they occur.

An example of a call purchase, with defined profit and loss zones, is shown in Figure 3.5. In this example, you buy one May 40 call for 2 ($-$ $200). In order to profit from this strategy, the call's value must increase to a point greater than the striking price *and* the cost of the option. In this case, you invested $200. So $42 per share is your break-even point. Time value will deteriorate between the purchase date and expiration, so increases must occur rapidly or they must consist of intrinsic value.

Even for buying a call that will expire within a few months, you should know in advance what risks you take and how much price movement will be needed to yield a profit.

Example: You have been tracking a stock with the idea of buying calls. Right now, you could get a call

loss zone: the price range of the underlying stock in which the option investor will lose (A limited loss occurs for a call buyer between the striking price and the break-even price; otherwise, the loss zone is any stock price lower than the option's striking price.)

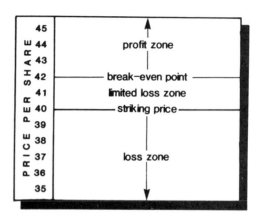

Figure 3.5.   Example of call purchase.

with a striking price of $40. It would cost you 2
($200). The stock's market value is $38, or $2 per
share out of the money. In deciding whether or not
to buy this call, you realize that, between now and
expiration, the stock will have to rise by at least 4
points—2 points to get to the striking price and
another 2 points to build some intrinsic value. If
this occurs by the expiration date, the option will
be worth exactly what you would have to pay for
it today. Remember, when the entire premium is
time value, you will need to offset that value with
intrinsic value or, if the demand for the option is
high, with yet more time value. You might con-
clude in this case that spending $200 is unwise.

Example: Another stock you have been following
has an option with a premium of 1 ($100), and is
currently at the money. Expiration is three months
away and the stock is now only 1 point away from
the break-even point. Considering these circumstances, you might decide the potential profit is
worth the risk.

In the first example, a break-even point was actually 4 points away: 2 points to get to the striking price and another 2 points to offset the premium cost. In the second example, only 2 points of stock movement are required to achieve the same thing. And the risk is only $100, or half as much as the risk in the first example.

You can make as much profit with a well-planned $100 investment as you can with an equally valuable $200 investment. However, when the cost *and* the risk are both higher, the best course is obvious.

Before buying any options, you need to also evaluate the underlying stock's attributes. These include price, dividend rate, volatility, and other features that, collectively, define the stock's safety. There is no point in selecting what seems a good option stock if, in fact, the stock itself will not perform well. At the very least, you should determine from recent history how responsive the stock is likely to be to the general movements in the market as a whole.

It is also wise to evaluate the entire market before taking a position in stock and options. Timing may be critical. For example, do you believe the market has recently risen at too fast a rate? If so, do you expect a correction? Perhaps you would do well to wait it out until you believe that conditions are better for buying. The problem is that all of these judgments are opinion only, and you might be wrong. The entire process of buying and selling in the market is based on opinion, timing, and judgment. See Chapter 6 for a more expanded discussion of stock selection.

Beyond the points of stock and option analysis, you need to be willing to live with the time factor. Your call will expire within a few months, meaning you have only a very limited time for that option to accumulate value. And any time value in the option today must be offset by the stock's price well before expiration.

In the next chapter, strategies for buying puts are examined and explained in depth.

CHAPTER 4

Buying Puts

You will recall that call buyers have the right to *buy* 100 shares of an underlying stock. A put grants the buyer the opposite right: to *sell* 100 shares of stock. The premium paid to acquire a put grants that right to you as the buyer. On the opposite side of the transaction is a seller who has agreed to buy 100 shares of the stock if you exercise the put.

As a put buyer, you have a choice to make in the near future. You may sell the put before it expires; you may exercise the put and sell 100 shares of the stock; or you may let the put expire worthless.

You are not obligated to sell 100 shares just because you own the put. You have the right to do so. The seller, however, would be obligated in the event you exercised your put. The decision you make as a put owner depends on the same points that motivate call owners. These include:

• The movement in the underlying stock and how that movement affects the put's premium value.
• Your motives for purchasing the put, and how today's market conditions affect that motive.
• Your willingness to wait out a series of events between now and expiration and your willing-

ness to wait and see what happens, versus the desire for a sure profit today.

UNDERSTANDING THE LIMITED LIFE OF THE PUT

Puts can be purchased strictly on speculation. If you believe the underlying stock will be worthless in the near future, you can either sell the stock short or buy a put.

Short selling of stock is a strategy employed by investors who believe the stock's value will fall. If they are correct, they will be able to close the position by buying the stock at a lower price. A short seller borrows the stock from the brokerage firm and then sells it. The brokerage firm demands a deposit of a portion of the stock's market value at the time of the short sale. If the stock's market value rises, the brokerage firm requires that more money be put on account.

The entire amount of the stock's market value is at risk, because the investor must make a deposit and must pay interest to the brokerage firm for the difference between the deposit and the market value. In that respect, selling short requires the same level of investment risk as buying stock.

Selling stock short is a very risky strategy with unlimited risk. A short seller hopes to gain from a price decline. But if the timing is wrong and the stock goes up instead of down, the seller will lose money.

Example: You have been watching a specific stock over the past few months. You believe it is overpriced today and that market value will fall in the near future. So you instruct your broker to sell short 100 shares. A few weeks pass and the stock has fallen 8 points. You call your broker again and place a closing purchase transaction to buy 100 shares of stock. Because the price today is lower than when you sold, you realize a profit of $800 (before brokerage fees).

Example: You sold short a stock last month when it was selling at $59 per share. At the time, you believed the stock was overpriced and that it would decline in value. However, a few days ago another company announced a tender offer for the company at $75 per share. The stock immediately rose to $73. If you enter a closing purchase transaction now, you will lose $1400 before brokerage fees (the difference between your initial sales price and current market value). If the tender offer is accepted, or if the stock rises for any other reason, you will eventually have to take the loss.

Instead of taking the risks of selling short, you can benefit from a stock's decline by buying puts and limit the risk in case your timing is wrong.

The limit of risk is a positive feature of buying puts. However, the put—like all options—will exist for a limited amount of time. If the strategy is to be profitable, price movement in the underlying stock must occur before expiration date. And the movement must be significant enough to surpass the amount you pay in premium. That movement must occur before expiration. So a put buyer trades limited risk for limited life.

Understanding the potential benefits is only half of the equation necessary if you are to succeed as a put buyer. You must also understand the risk and know how much price movement in the underlying stock will be needed to produce a profit.

Too many speculators buy puts with high time value and thus require many points of decline in the stock's value in order to profit. If the stock is fairly stable in its price movement, the chances of profit are greatly reduced.

Buying puts is suitable for you only if you understand these risks and if you are familiar with the price history of the underlying stock. You must also be able and willing to lose the entire put premium.

Example: An investor has $600 available to invest and believes that the market as a whole will fall in the near future. One problem, however: She cannot afford to lose the $600, which is her entire savings account. She buys two puts valued at 3, spending the entire $600. The market does fall as she predicted; however, the stock on which she purchased puts is not affected all that much, and she is not able to realize a profit. At expiration date, the puts are worth 1 point each. She sells and receives $200.

This investor's perception of the market was correct. Prices fell. But the puts were not profitable, because the stock was too stable to produce a profit in a limited period of time. In addition, puts were not appropriate for this individual. She could not afford the loss.

The investor in this example failed to analyze the market and the feasibility of buying puts. She saw only the potential for gain and did not consider the potential for loss. She also ignored the strength of the underlying stock. If it is unlikely to decline in value quickly enough to produce a profit, put buying is a poor idea.

If you understand the risks and can afford to speculate, put buying might have a place in your portfolio.

Example: An experienced investor has a portfolio that is well diversified. He owns several stocks, shares in two mutual funds, and real estate. He has been investing for a number of years and fully understands the risks involved in various markets. He considers his portfolio as a long-term investment and is not all that concerned with short-term price movements. He also has several hundred dollars available for speculation and believes the market will fall. So he buys puts with the money, selecting stocks that, in his opinion, are likely to fall enough to produce a profit.

This individual understands the risks involved in speculation and already has built a base in his portfolio. Diversifying with a portion of his capital is appropriate so long as he understands the risks and is willing and able to lose money. With that risk in mind, he takes the chance, hoping for a short-term profit.

In addition, he can afford the loss. The money used to buy puts is above and beyond the longer-term portfolio values the investor has already built up. Being able to afford the loss, understanding the market, and selecting stocks and puts intelligently all add up to a greater likelihood of success.

JUDGING THE PUT

Time works against all option buyers. Not only will your option expire in a few months, but you must also accept the declining time value of the put.

You can select a low-priced put—one that is out of the money—and will need many points of price movement for a profit. Or you can select a put that is in the money. In that case, if the stock moves in the wrong direction, you stand to lose more.

Example: You bought a put and paid a premium of 5 ($500). At that time, the stock's market value was 4 points below the striking price, or in the money by 4 points. (You will recall that for calls, "in the money" means the stock's value is higher than the striking price; it is opposite for a put.) However, by the time of expiration, the stock had risen 4½ points and the option was worth only ½ ($50). The time value had completely disappeared, and you sold on the last day possible. Your loss: $450.

Example: You bought a put several months ago, paying a premium of ½ ($50). At that time, the stock's value was 5 points above the striking price, or out of the money. At the time of expiration, the stock's market value declined 4½ points, meaning it is ½ point in the money. Its value is also ½ or $50. By selling at that point, you break even before transaction fees. In other words, you will lose on a net basis, because you are assessed a fee at time of purchase and another at time of sale.

The problem is not limited to picking the right direction the underlying stock will move. The degree of movement must be great enough to produce a profit within the limited time before expiration of the put.

Some speculators attempt to bargain hunt in the options market. The belief, apparently, is that a cheap option is a better buy than an expensive one; but this is not necessarily the case. The question of quality should be considered as well, as with all purchases. Some options that are low-priced are also low-quality. This means your chances for profit are correspondingly low. All options purchasers should examine the reasons that a particular option is priced at a "bargain" level. It might reflect its true value, and might not be a bargain at all.

Example: You bought a put last week when it was in the money and paid $600. You believed the stock was overpriced and was likely to fall. Two days after your purchase, the stock fell 1 point. At that time, you sold and received $700. That is a return of your $600 investment plus a $100 profit. That profit represents a return of 16.7 percent in two days (before transaction fees).

You need to set goals for yourself whenever you speculate in puts. Do not allow the "greed factor" to take over. Identify in advance when you will sell. That means limiting losses and recognizing what you consider a target gain.

Example: You bought a put last month and paid a premium of 4 ($400). At that time, you decided to set a few goals for yourself. First, you decided that if the put's value fell by 2 points, you would sell and accept the loss of $200. Second, you promised yourself that if the put's value rose by 3 points or more, you would sell immediately and take your profit. In short, you decided you were willing to accept a 50 percent loss, but would also close out the position if you could get a 75 percent gain.

Setting goals is the only way to succeed if you plan to speculate in options. Too many speculators fall into the no-win trap because they fail to set standards for themselves.

Example: You bought a put last month and paid 5 ($500). Your plan was to sell if the value went up 2 points or more. A week after your purchase, the stock's market value fell and the put's value went up to 8 ($800)—an increase of 3 points. You didn't sell, though, because you thought the stock's market value might continue to fall. If that happened, your put would be even more valuable, and you didn't want to lose any future profits. The week after that, the stock's value rose by 4 points and the put lost a corresponding value. The opportunity was lost.

The lost opportunity might not repeat, so potential profits are not taken. The same logic applies when a put option loses value.

Example: You bought a put last month, paying a premium of 6 ($600), and resolved that you would sell if its value fell by 2 points or more. A couple of weeks ago, the stock rose and the put's value declined to your bail-out target. You hesitated, though, hoping the stock's value would fall back. However, as of today, the stock has risen a total of 5 points, and your $600 investment is now worth only $100.

Even if the stock does eventually fall, time is still working against you. The longer it takes for the turnaround in value, the more time value you lose. The stock could fall a point or two over a three-month period, in which case you will be trading time value for intrinsic value. You might never get back to an acceptable minimal loss level.

The problem of time value is the same problem that call buyers experience. With puts, a decline in the value of the underlying stock is advantageous. See Figure 4.1.

Example: You buy a put for a premium of 5 ($500) with a striking price of 30. Between purchase date and expiration, the underlying stock rises above the striking price but then falls to 27, which is 3 points below. If you sell the put at expiration you will lose $200, because time value has gone out of the put. Even though the stock is 3 points in the money, it was not enough to yield a profit.

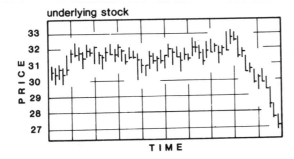

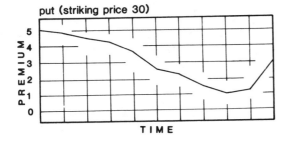

Figure 4.1.   Diminishing time value of the put relative to the underlying stock.

The further out of the money a stock is, the cheaper the premium for a put—and the lower the chance for profit. And the further in the money a stock is, the more expensive the put, because you will be paying both for time and intrinsic value.

If you buy an in-the-money put and the underlying stock increases in value, you will lose $1 of premium value for every point of movement. And of course, you gain $1 for every point of decline.

Whether you prefer lower premium puts that are out of the money or in-the-money puts that cost more, be aware of the number of points between the stock's current value and the striking price. The more points away, the greater is your risk.

To minimize this risk, limit your speculation to within 5 points from the striking price. As shown in Figure 4.2, you should avoid deep in and deep out puts, as they will either be too expensive or too far away from a profitable price level.

Set goals and stay with them. Consider the premium value, the mix of time and intrinsic value, the time until expiration, and the price movement and strength of the underlying stock. Do not make the most common speculator's mistake: shopping for a put based only on premium bargains and time until expiration. Look at the entire picture, and remember that there is an inescapable relationship between the stock and the put. Volatility and perceptions of that company by the investing public

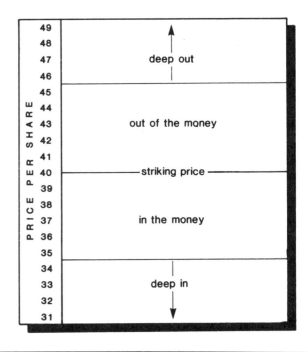

Figure 4.2. Deep in/deep out puts.

will determine how your put will perform between purchase and expiration.

ESTABLISHING GOALS

There are three reasons to buy puts. The first is purely speculative: the hope of realizing a substantial profit in a short period of time. Second, you can buy puts to avoid the risks of short selling. Third, puts can serve as a form of insurance against declines in stock you own.

Goal 1: Gaining Leverage

Most investors who buy puts are hoping to profit from leverage. With a limited amount of money available, the potential for profits is greater with puts than it is in selling stock short. And the risks are also limited.

Here's how leverage works in the case of puts. A stock is currently valued at $62 per share. If you sell it short and it falls 5 points, you can close the position and realize a $500 gain. If you believe the stock will fall and instead of selling it short, you buy 12 puts (total $6000), your potential for profit is greater. A drop of 5 points will yield a $6000 gain, or a 100 percent return, assuming that no time value is lost.

If you do not have a lot of capital available to make the choice between selling stock and buying puts, you can still use leverage to your advantage.

Example: You buy a put for a premium of 5 ($500) with a striking price of 60. The stock is currently selling at $60 per share. Aware of the risks and the potential rewards of this strategy, you compare leverage to the potential rewards and risks of selling short 100 shares. As shown in Figure 4.3, a drop of 5 points in the stock would produce a $500 gain with either strategy.

Because a short sale requires the combination of a deposit of part of the stock's value with the brokerage firm as well as interest payments on the difference, the short seller is just as committed to the value of the stock as a buyer would be. So any comparison of yields should be based on an understanding that short sellers are at risk for 100 shares of stock.

A decline of 5 points produces an 8.1 percent profit to the short seller and a 100 percent yield to the put buyer. For that difference in yield, compare the risks. The short seller's risks are unlimited; the stock could rise to any level. The put buyer's risk is limited to the $500 paid for the premium. A drop

	STOCK (1)		PUT (2)	
	PROFIT OR LOSS	RATE OF RETURN	PROFIT OR LOSS	RATE OF RETURN
price decrease of 5 points	$500	8.1%	$500	100%
price decrease of 1 point	$100	1.6%	$100	20%
no price change	0	0	0	0
price increase of 1 point	−$100	−1.6%	−$100	− 20%
price increase of 5 points	−$500	−8.1%	−$500	−100%

(1) sold short at $62 per share ($6 200)

(2) striking price 60, premium 5 ($500)

Figure 4.3.   Rates of return: selling short versus buying puts.

of 1 point in value of the stock will produce a 1.6 percent profit to the short seller and a 20 percent profit to the put buyer.

Losses can be compared on a similar basis. When a short seller's stock rises in value, the loss can be substantial. But the amount of loss for the put buyer is limited to the amount paid for the put.

Most put buyers never intend to exercise the put. If puts increase in value, the put is sold for a higher price than its purchase value.

Goal 2: Limiting Risks

It is possible to double your money in a very short period of time by speculating in puts. And the leveraging of your money increases even a modest investment's potential. In one respect, leverage increases risks; in another, it decreases risks.

Risks are increased with leverage because you could lose the entire amount invested. The more you invest in puts, the more you stand to gain—or to lose.

Example: You recently bought a put and paid a premium of 4 ($400). However, expiration date is coming up soon and the stock's market value has risen above the striking price. If the put expires, you will stand to lose your entire $400. Time has worked against you. You know that the stock's market value might eventually fall below the striking price, but not necessarily in time to save your put's value.

Risks are decreased when your alternative is selling short. If a stock rises instead of falling as you expect, your puts will decline in value. But if you sell short, you must make up the difference when you close the short position. And that could be many thousands of dollars more than you'd planned.

Example: An investor sold short 200 shares of a stock with market value of $45 per share. The stock later rises in value to $52 and, fearing further price increases, the investor sells. His loss: $1400. If the same investor had bought puts instead of selling short, the potential loss would have been limited to the total premium paid. The fear of further price increases in the stock would not have been a factor. The short seller's potential loss is unlimited. The put buyer can never lose more than the amount placed at risk.

Some investors prefer short selling over buying puts because there is no time pressure involved. A put will expire within nine months, while a short position can be left open indefinitely. So long as the short seller is able to keep the required deposit on account with the brokerage firm, and so long as that investor is willing to pay interest on the difference between the deposit and current market value, the short position does not expire like an option.

The risks of a short position can be reduced by buying calls, as explained in the last chapter. Of course, calls also expire, so to maintain protection of a short position, the investor must be willing to replace one call with another as expiration occurs. Buying calls to protect a short position adds to the cost and requires greater declines in value to produce a profit.

If you believe a stock's value will fall, the alternative of buying puts makes sense. The risk of loss is limited, and your broker will not require that you deposit a large sum of money to cover a short sale.

For the convenience of having leverage, you must be able to accept losses when stock goes up instead of down. You must also be willing to accept the disadvantage of time. Your put will expire in a few months. Every put buyer has the added disadvantage of time value premium. As expiration nears, that value disappears from the option, even when the stock does not rise in price.

Goal 3: Hedging a Long Position

Put buying is not always purely speculative. A very conservative strategy involves buying one put for every 100 shares of the underlying stock you buy as a way of protecting yourself from declines in price. Each put is known as a *married put* since it is tied to the underlying stock.

The risk of decline in price is a constant concern of every investor. If you buy stock and it falls in value, you might sell, fearing further declines. Or you might hold onto it, hoping for a rebound. It could take months or even years for a stock to recover from a severe decline. For protection against such declines, you buy puts as a form of insurance, which is known as a *hedge* strategy. In the event of a decline in value of the stock, you can exercise the put and sell your stock through exercise. This action is called *put to seller*.

Example: You own 100 shares of stock, which you bought at $57 per share. You bought the stock because it is volatile, and you know it could rise or fall dramatically in a fairly short period of time. The potential for gain is significant; so is the potential for loss. To protect yourself against the consequences of a loss in market value, you decide to buy a put on the underlying stock. You spend $100

married put: descriptive of a hedge position when a put and 100 shares are bought at the same time (The put is "married" to the 100 shares on which the downside protection is provided.)

hedge: a strategy in which one position protects the other (Buying a put is a form of hedge to protect the value of 100 shares of the underlying stock.)

put to seller: the action that occurs when a put buyer exercises the put (The 100 shares of stock are sold—put—to the seller at the striking price.)

and buy a put with a striking price of $50. Two months later, the stock has declined to $36 per share, and your put is near expiration. The put has a current value of 14 ($1400).

In this situation, you have two choices.

1. Sell the put, and realize a $1300 profit. Your original cost of the investment was $58 per share (purchase price of $57, plus 1 point to buy the put). Your net cost is $45 ($5800 investment, less $1300 profit on the put). Your basis is now 9 points above current market value. If the stock increases in value, you will realize a profit once it exceeds the $45 level. Without the put, your basis would be 21 points above current market value.

2. Exercise the put, and sell the stock for $50 per share. In this instance, you sell for 8 points below your original cost. You will lose the $100 paid for the insurance provided by the put, plus commissions on the stock purchase and upon exercise of the option.

Regardless of the choice you make, you end up better off than if you had simply purchased the stock without the protection of the put. You either cut the amount of loss following a severe decline in the underlying stock's value, or you realize a profit on the put while keeping the stock.

The two choices—exercising or selling the put—both result in losses. Remember, though, that without the put, the loss in the stock would be severe. It's better to lose a little than to lose a lot, and a put can be used to protect your position in a stock to that degree.

Downside protection takes away from your potential for gain. The money invested in the put's premium will reduce future profits in the event the

downside protection: a strategy involving the purchase of one put for every 100 shares owned, as a form of insurance (Every point drop in the stock is matched by an increase of 1 point in the put.)

stock rises, but that reduction is limited. Of greater concern should be the limit on the downside.

In the event the stock's value rises, your potential losses are frozen to the amount of the put's premium and no more. Whether you exercise the put or sell it at a profit, downside protection helps you establish an acceptable level of loss and to fix that loss for the duration of the put's life.

Example: You recently purchased 100 shares of stock at $60 per share. At the same time, you bought a put with a striking price of 60, paying a premium of 3 ($300). The total amount invested is $6300. Before making your purchases, you analyzed the potential profit or loss and concluded that your losses would never exceed 4.8 percent ($300 paid for the put, divided by $6300, the total amount you spent).

You also recognize that an increase in the stock's value of 3 points or less is not a profit at all. Your total basis is $6300 (combining the stock purchase with the call premium). So profits do not begin to accrue until the stock's value exceeds $63 per share.

A summary of this analysis is shown in Figure 4.4. Note that regardless of the severity of decline in the stock's price, the loss never exceeds 4.8 percent of the total amount invested. That's because, for every point the stock falls in value, the option gains a point of intrinsic value.

DEFINING PROFIT ZONES

To decide whether buying a put is a reasonable move to make, always be aware of potential profits and losses. Pay special attention to the number of points the stock must move to produce profits,

PRICE MOVEMENT, UNDERLYING STOCK	PROFIT OR LOSS		NET PROFIT OR LOSS (3)	
	STOCK (1)	PUT (2)	AMOUNT	RATE
down 20 points	-$2,000	$1,700	-$ 300	- 4.8%
down 5 points	-$ 500	$ 200	-$ 300	- 4.8%
down 3 points	-$ 300	0	-$ 300	- 4.8%
no change	0	-$ 300	-$ 300	- 4.8%
up 3 points	$ 300	-$ 300	0	0
up 5 points	$ 500	-$ 300	$ 200	3.2%
up 20 points	$2,000	-$ 300	$1,700	27.0%

(1) stock purchased at $60 per share
(2) put striking price 60, premium 3
(3) return based on total cost of $6300

Figure 4.4.   Downside protection: selling short versus buying puts.

while also keeping in mind the time you have until expiration.

Comparing limited losses to potential profits when using puts for downside protection is one analysis that will help you determine the value of buying a put. And when trying to pick a sound speculative investment, the time until expiration and the distance between current stock value and the striking price—as well as time value—will help you identify a worthwhile risk.

The profit and loss zones for puts are the reverse of the same zones for a call. When you buy a call, you hope for a rise in the stock's price. But as a put buyer, you will profit if the value of the stock falls. See Figure 4.5.

buy one put for 3:

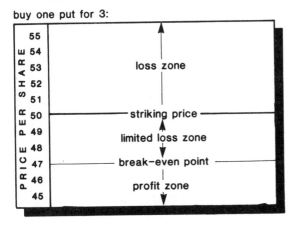

Figure 4.5.   A put's profit and loss zones.

Example: You buy a put with a striking price of 50 and pay a premium of 3 ($300). Your break-even point is $47 per share. Once the stock falls to that level, it will have intrinsic value equal to the premium you paid. Your put can be sold between $47 and $50 per share for a limited loss. And if the price goes above the striking price of $50 per share, the put will be worthless at the point of expiration.

Before buying any put, determine the profit, loss, and break-even zones. For the money you will be placing at risk, how much price movement will be needed to yield a profit? How much time will you have? And is the risk worth taking?

An example of a put purchase, with defined profit and loss zones, is shown in Figure 4.6. In this example, you buy one May 40 put for 3 (−$300). The outcome of this strategy is the exact opposite of buying a call. You will profit if the value of stock falls below the striking price of 40. However, the point decline must be greater than your

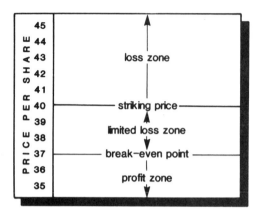

Figure 4.6.   Example of put purchase.

purchase price by expiration; otherwise, the put will be worth less than the $300 invested. Like call purchasing, time works against you when you buy puts. They will expire within a short number of months. However, risk is limited to the amount spent on premium.

The mistake most investors make is failing to set any standards for themselves. You should plan to cut your losses at a specific level and to sell your put once you realize an acceptable amount of profit.

Remember the important points to evaluate in buying puts:

• Your motive (leverage, reduction of risk, or downside protection).
• The premium and amount of time value.
• Time until expiration.
• Distance between the stock's current market value and the striking price.
• The number of points needed to yield a profit.
• Characteristics of the underlying stock. (Chap-

6 provides guidelines for selecting stocks appropriate to your option strategy.)

Option buyers stand to earn impressive percentage gains in a short period of time, but must also live with the disadvantage of time. On the other side are sellers of options. Time is on their side for the same reason it is against the buyer: The time value in a premium diminishes as expiration date approaches. So the seller benefits from diminishing values to the same degree that the buyer loses. The next chapter explains strategies and risks of selling calls.

CHAPTER 5

Selling Calls

M ost of us think about investing in a precise
sequence. First, you buy a security. Then, at
some later date, you sell. If the sales price is higher
than the purchase price, you realize a profit. If it is
lower, you suffer a loss. However, when you become a call seller, this common sequence is reversed.

If you buy a call and later sell it (see Chapter 3),
that is a transaction conforming to the common
sequence. In this chapter we explain how to sell
calls as the first step, and purchase them later. The
outcome is the same as with the usual sequence. If
the purchase price is lower than the sales price, you
realize a profit; if the purchase price is higher, you
suffer a loss.

By starting out selling the option, you are paid
at the time the transaction is initiated. You pay for
the purchase later on (or, if the option expires, you
never pay a purchase price, and you still keep the
sale proceeds).

If this all sounds too good to be true, remember
that selling calls involves very special risks. We will
explain these risks as we proceed through the chapter. You will see that some forms of call selling are
extremely risky, while others are very conservative.

Call sellers enjoy significant and important advantages over call buyers. The last two chapters gave several examples of how time works against you. Even if the underlying stock moves in the desired direction, time value deterioriates as expiration approaches. This buyer disadvantage is a seller's advantage.

Because time value evaporates, time is on the seller's side. The buyer's greatest problem—disappearing time value—is the seller's greatest benefit. At the time you initiate a sale (the opening transaction), you want the highest possible time value. You sell the option in the hope that time value will disappear. Remember, because you sell the option *before* you buy it, you want its value to decline. Then you can buy the option at a lower price in the future.

By selling a call, you grant the buyer the right to buy 100 shares of the underlying stock at the striking price, and at any time prior to expiration.

Most investment strategies are identified specifically by risk characteristics. These are clearly identified and should be understood by anyone undertaking the strategy. The definition of most strategies involves attributes that are unchanging. For example, the risks of buying stocks or bonds are consistent from one moment to another. A knowledgeable investor understands this and accepts the consistency of risk. But call selling can be highly conservative or highly risky, depending on how the strategy is undertaken. It is one of the few investment strategies offering you an extreme on either end of the risk spectrum.

SELLING UNCOVERED CALLS

If you sell a call when you do not own 100 shares, you are taking a great risk. In fact, this type of sale is one of the highest forms of risk an investor can take: a short position with unlimited potential for loss.

Remembering that the short position grants a buyer the right to buy 100 shares at the striking price, you must be prepared to deliver those shares if the call is exercised. If you do not own those shares, you will be required upon exercise to buy them at the current market value and then sell them at the striking price.

Example: You enter into an uncovered call position when the underlying stock's market value is $44 per share. The April 45 call's premium is 5 ($500). You don't own shares of this stock. You sell the April 45 call and your brokerage firm adds $500 to your account (less transaction fee). Before the option expires, the stock unexpectedly soars to $71 per share, and your option is exercised by the buyer. You will lose $2100 (current market value of $71, less the striking price of $45, and less the $500 premium you were paid for selling the call):

Current market value	$ 7100
Less striking price	(4500)
Less call premium	(500)
Loss	$ 2100

When you do not own 100 shares and a call is exercised, you are required to deliver and must, therefore, buy those shares at the current value. Because market value is determined by demand, the per-share price is potentially unlimited.

The risk of selling calls in this manner is extreme. Because of this, your broker will allow you to sell calls only if you meet specific requirements. These normally include having enough value in your brokerage account to provide some protection in the event of an exceptionally high loss. Then the firm could sell shares of stock to cover the loss if you were not able to do so. You also need to be approved in advance just to sell calls. The brokerage firm is required to determine that you understand the risks involved, and that you have the resources *and* the experience to take those risks.

The requirement that your portfolio include stocks, cash, and other assets is one form of *margin* requirement imposed by your broker. Such requirements apply not only to option transactions but also to buying or selling stocks through borrowing of funds from the brokerage firm.

When you enter into a sale transaction, you are referred to as the writer. The call writer hopes that the value of the underlying stock will remain at or below the striking price. If that hope is realized, the option will expire worthless. And it is worth remembering that the break-even point (without considering brokerage costs) is equal to the striking price plus the number of points received for selling the call.

margin: an account with a brokerage firm that contains a minimum, required amount of cash or securities to provide collateral for short positions or for purchases made and not paid for until sold

Example: You sold a call with a striking price of $35, and were paid a premium of 3 ($300). Before deducting brokerage fees, your break-even point is $38 per share: the striking price of $35 plus $300 (3 points) you received when you sold the call.

As a *writer*, you have the right to cancel your open position at any time you want before expiration and before exercise. This is achieved by purchasing the option. Remember, if you are the writer, you initiated the position by selling the call; you close the position by later purchasing the same option. If time value declines or the underlying stock's market value falls, or if both of these events take place, you will be able to cancel your open position at a price lower than the sales price. The result: profit.

writer: the individual who sells—writes—a call

Example: You sold a call two months ago and were paid a premium of 3 ($300). The underlying stock's market value has remained below the striking price, even though it has not changed much during the time you have had the open position. But time value has shrunk enough that you now have a choice. You can close the position by purchasing the option at a lower price, or you can wait for expiration and keep the entire amount of premium as profit. Purchasing now ensures the profit in the option today. Waiting for expiration continues your risk exposure but will also result in more profit.

Whenever you sell a call and you do not own 100 or more shares of the underlying stock, the option is called a *naked* or *uncovered option*. And remember, your risk in a *naked position* is not just limited to the option's status at the point of expiration. The buyer has the right to exercise the call at any time.

naked option: an option that is sold to create an open position, when the seller does not own 100 shares of the underlying stock

uncovered option: the same as a naked option, or the opposite of a covered option (when a call is sold and the investor also owns 100 shares)

naked position: the status when the seller does not own 100 shares of the underlying stock, but has sold a call

Example: You sold a naked call last week, and the underlying stock went into the money as of yesterday. But there are another four months to go until expiration so you are not worried. However, your broker called this morning and advised you that the call was exercised. You are now required to buy 100 shares of stock, and the option no longer exists.

Most calls are not exercised early, but it does happen. You cannot predict whether or not a specific call will be exercised, since buyers and sellers are not matched up one to one. The Options Clearing Corporation (OCC) acts as buyer to every seller and as seller to every buyer. When a buyer exercises, that order is assigned at random to a seller. You won't even know it has happened until your broker informs you that your call has been assigned.

In order to profit from selling calls, the underlying stock must do one of two things.

1. It must remain at or below the striking price, so that it will expire worthless.
2. It must remain at a stable enough price so that the option can later be purchased for a lower premium due to a decline in time value.

The profit and loss zones for uncovered calls are shown in Figure 5.1. Because you receive cash for selling the option, the break-even point is higher than the striking price. In this example, a call is sold for 5, hence the break-even point (not considering stock or option commissions) is 5 points above the striking price.

Your brokerage firm will require you to put on

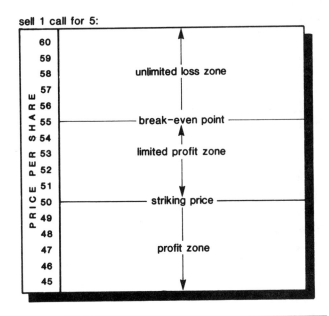

Figure 5.1. An uncovered call's profit and loss zones.

deposit a percentage of the total potential liability for writing calls. For example, you write one call with a striking price of $40. If the call is exercised, you will have to sell 100 shares at $40 per share. But at that time, the stock could have a market value of $45, $50, or $80 per share.

Many of the huge losses investors experienced in October of 1987 resulted from excessive margin activity, some involving calls or puts or both. Even the brokerage firms did not anticipate the degree of potential loss that resulted. Consequently, many brokerage firms no longer permit the public to write options on margin. If you want to take such a large risk, you will be limited in the amount and degree the brokerage firm will allow. To protect against large losses, you will have to pledge securities already in your account. Different rules may be applied to institutional funders, such as pension plans, mutual funds, and insurance companies.

Example: You have advised your broker that you intend to write uncovered calls. Your portfolio is currently valued at $20,000 in stocks and cash. Your broker will restrict your uncovered call writing activity to a level that, in their estimation, would not exceed maximum losses of $20,000. However, if market conditions change and your portfolio value declines, you could be forced to either deposit more money or close some uncovered positions.

Example: You would like to write (sell) puts as part of your investment strategy. You have stocks and cash valued at $20,000. Your brokerage firm will restrict you to positions that would not exceed a $20,000 commitment in the event of exercise. However, because you will be writing puts and not calls, the potential for loss is much more limited.

The point here is that writing puts involves a

limited loss, since the very worst outcome is that a stock's value could decline to zero. There is a finite "worst case" loss. This is not true for uncovered calls, where losses could be extremely high if stocks rise far beyond your expectations—especially if you have many uncovered calls at the same time.

SELLING COVERED CALLS

In comparison to the high risks of selling uncovered calls, the covered call write is a very conservative strategy. In this case, you *cover* yourself by owning 100 shares of the underlying stock for each call you sell.

There are several advantages to the *covered option*.

1. You are paid a premium for each option you sell, which is cash placed into your account. While this is also true for uncovered options, the same risks do not apply. You can afford exercise because you already own the stock.

2. The true net price of your stock is reduced by the value of the option premium. It is a form of discount, because you are paid for selling the option. This gives you more flexibility, more downside protection, and more versatility for selling options with high time value.

3. Selling covered calls provides you with the freedom to accept moderate interim price declines, because the premium received has reduced the price. Simply owning the stock without discounting through option sales means that even a moderate decline represents a paper loss.

cover: descriptive of the status when an investor is long in the stock and short in a call option (For each option contract sold, the investor owns 100 shares.)

covered option: a call option that is sold to create an open position, when the investor has 100 shares to cover the short option position

Example: You have 100 shares of stock, which you purchased last year at $50 per share. Current market value is $54. You would be willing to sell this stock at a profit. Accordingly, you write a November 55 call option and receive a premium of 5 ($500). Once this is done, your real basis in the stock is $45 (original cost of $5000, reduced by $500 for the option premium). If the stock's market value were to remain anywhere between $45 and $54 per share, your investment will still be profitable; in addition, the call will not be exercised. So long as the option is out of the money, you are free to buy it and cancel the position at any time.

One of three events can take place when you sell a call for every 100 shares you own: an increase in price, a decrease in price, or no significant change. As long as you own 100 shares of stock, any dividends will be paid to you, whether you sell options or not. The value of writing covered calls should be compared to the value of simply buying and holding stock, as shown in Table 5.1.

Before any strategy is undertaken, you should understand the advantages and disadvantages, including the sacrifice of potential profits.

lock in: condition of the underlying security when the investor has an offsetting short call (so long as the call is open, the writer is locked into the striking price, regardless of current market value of the stock; in the event of exercise, the stock must be delivered at that locked-in price.)

A call seller can *lock in* the price of the underlying stock if the call is exercised. Regardless of how significantly the stock rises, the seller will receive only the striking price value upon exercise.

CALCULATING RATE OF RETURN

If your purpose in owning stock is to hold it for many years, writing calls is not an appropriate strategy. The call writer's objective is a different one. It is to produce consistent yields from the combination of three sources of income:

- Call premium.
- Limited capital gains on stock.
- Dividends.

Table 5.1. Comparing Strategies

| | Outcomes | |
| | --- | --- |
Event	Owning Stock and Writing Calls	Owning Stock Only
Stock goes up in value	Call if exercised; profits are limited to striking price and call premium.	Stock can be sold at a profit.
Stock remains at or below the striking price	Time value declines; the call can be closed out at a profit or allowed to expire worthless.	No profit or loss until sold.
Stock declines in value	Stock price is discounted by call premium; the call is closed or allowed to expire worthless.	Loss on the stock.
Dividends	Earned while stock is held.	Earned while stock is held.

Example: You purchased 100 shares of stock and paid $32 per share. Several months later, the stock's market value had risen to $38. You wrote a March 35 call. Your reasoning: Since your basis in the stock was $32, having to sell at $35 would still be profitable. And because you receive cash for selling the option, you get additional profit as well. In this case, the option you sold produced a premium of 8 ($800). At the time you sold the call, you realized that if exercised, your total profit would be $1100 ($300 from stock appreciation and $800 from call premium). Two months after you sold the call, the stock's market value rose to $65 per share, and the call was exercised. Your profit is frozen at $1100 because you locked yourself into the striking price of $35 per share.

This example illustrates the *potential* lost profit that option writers have to accept. Simply owning

discount: a benefit of selling covered calls (The true price of the stock is reduced by the amount of premium received: If the basis in stock is $30 per share and an option is sold for a premium of 5, the basis is discounted to $25 per share.)

total return: the combination of income from the call premium, capital gains in the stock, and any dividends received (Total return should be computed in two ways: if the option is exercised and if it expires worthless.)

the stock—without writing any calls—would have produced a profit of $3300. Covered call writers literally limit the amount of profit they can earn. In exchange for this, the call premium paid to the writer represents certainty. The profit is ensured but limited.

What are the chances of a stock soaring in price? It does happen, but cannot be depended on. If you sell a call and later limit your profits, have you really lost?

You cannot lose profits you never had. One of the pitfalls in covered call writing is to regret the "loss" experienced in those rare cases when a stock does soar.

By accepting the limitation of writing covered calls, you do give up the potential for exceptional gains. But you also *discount* your price, which allows you to have some protection against moderate drops in stock values. You continue to receive dividends. And while you will miss out on the occasional spectacular rise, you settle for consistent and better-than-average rates of return.

A covered call writer should always identify both the profit and loss zones (shown in Figure 5.2) and also calculate the rate of return.

A covered call's profit and loss zone is determined by the combination of two factors: the option's premium value and the underlying stock's market value. If the stock falls below a break-even point (price paid, less option premium received), that's a loss. Of course, by owning stock, you enjoy the luxury of deciding when to sell, so you can hold stock until the price rebounds. A loss occurs only if you actually sell the stock.

You should never sell a call unless you will be completely satisfied in the event of exercise. For this reason, figuring out your *total return* before you sell a call is very important.

buy stock $50 per share,
sell 1 call for 5:

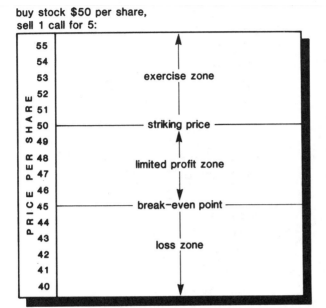

Figure 5.2.   A covered call's profit and loss zones.

Total return includes stock appreciation, call premium, and dividends. If the option expires worthless, you enjoy one rate of return; if you close the position by buying the option, your rate of return is different.

Example: You own 100 shares of stock that cost $41 per share. The current value is $44 per share, and you are considering selling a July 45 call. The premium is 5. Between now and expiration, you also expect to receive a total of $40 in dividends.

If the call in this example is exercised, the return will consist of all three elements.

Stock appreciation	$400
Call premium	500
Dividends	40
Total return	$940
Yield (on $4100)	22.9%

If the call is not exercised, but expires worthless, the total return does not include appreciation from the underlying stock. It is still held and will not produce a yield until sold. So return would be

Call premium	$500
Dividends	40
Total return	$540
Yield (on $4100)	13.2%

Although the yield in the second instance is lower, you still own the stock. So you are free to either sell it or write another call.

TIMING THE DECISION

A first-time call writer might be surprised to experience an immediate exercise. Exercise can occur at any time you are in the money, but you can assume that it will occur at or close to expiration, since that's true in most cases. Nevertheless, the call writer must be prepared to give up 100 shares of stock at any time from the day the call is written until the day of exercise.

As shown in Figure 5.3, during the life of a call, the underlying stock might swing several points above and below the striking price. If you own 100 shares and are considering selling a call, you should keep the following points in mind.

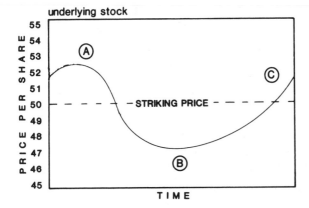

A in the money—best time
   to sell a call

B out of the money—best
   time to buy a call

C in the money at expiration
   —calls will be exercised

**Figure 5.3.   Timing of call transactions relative to
price movement of underlying stock.**

1. When the striking price of the call is higher than
the original cost of the stock, exercise is not
negative since you will profit from both price
appreciation and the call premium.
2. If you sell a call for a striking price below the
original cost of the stock, you should be sure
that the premium is greater than the loss you
will have in case of exercise.

Example: You bought 100 shares at $43 per share
and sell a call with a striking price of $40. If exer-
cised, you will lose $300 on the stock. So the pre-
mium should be greater than 3.

3. In calculating potential yields, you must be sure to allow for commission costs on stock and option upon purchase, sale, and exercise.
4. For the benefit of a consistent profit from writing calls, you give up the potential for larger gains in the event the stock's price rises.

Selecting an appropriate call depends on the price you originally pay, plus the current price of the stock. An option's premium at various price levels will further affect your decision.

Example: You purchase stock at $51 per share, and it is currently worth $53. Rather than sell the stock, you choose to sell a call with a striking price of $50 and receive a premium of 7 ($700).

The action in this example provides several benefits.

1. If the stock falls in value to below your purchase price, you can buy the option at a profit or allow it to expire worthless.
2. By selling the option, you discount your price from $51 to $44 and gain valuable downside protection if the stock's price declines.
3. You continue to receive dividends.

You might also choose to sell a call that is deep in the money.

Example: You purchased stock at $51 per share, and it is currently worth $53. You will receive at least $500 more by selling a 45 call. But that also increases the chance of exercise. And for the additional premium, you also give up points in the stock's value.

Purchase price	$ 5100
Exercise value	4500
Loss on the stock	$ (600)

If you receive 11 ($1100) for the call, your net profit will be reduced to only $500 in the event of exercise. You give up $600 by committing to a striking price 6 points below your original cost.

You should always select options and time your purchases with all of the following points in mind.

* Your original cost.
* Amount of the premium.
* Relationship of current value to striking price.
* Time until expiration.
* Total return if the call is exercised and if it expires worthless.
* Your objectives in owning the stock and in selling the call (immediate income, downside protection, or long-term growth).

AVOIDING EXERCISE

Assuming that you sell a call on stock you originally purchased because you considered it a worthwhile investment, you might then want to avoid exercise. You must be willing to live with the possibility that your call will be exercised. But many call writers can also benefit by taking action to either defer or completely avoid exercise.

There are several ways to avoid exercise. You cannot depend on an ideal movement in the price of the underlying stock, so you might find yourself in the money and near exercise.

First, to avoid exercise you can cancel an option position by purchasing it, even though you lose on the transaction. In some cases, this action is profitable despite the fact you accept a loss.

Example: You purchased stock at $21 per share and later sold a June 25 call, receiving a premium of 4. The stock is presently valued at $30 per share, and the option premium is at 6. If you buy the option, you will lose $200 on the transaction (original sale at a premium of 4, less closing purchase at 6). However, by avoiding exercise at the striking price of $25 per share, you now own stock with a current market value of $30, which is 3 points higher than your loss.

In selling the call, you had the advantage of downside protection. If the stock had fallen even to $17 per share, you would have been even (original stock at $21, less option premium of 4). But since the stock rose, closing out the option at a loss is a smart move. Considering the current market value of the stock in comparison to the striking price, you are ahead by making this decision. The stock is worth $30, but by closing the call position you free yourself from the commitment to deliver those shares for $25, which would mean a loss of $600.

Second, you can avoid exercise by exchanging one call for another and at the same time make a profit. Since the premium is higher for options that have a longer period of time to go until expiration, you gain the advantage of time value if you *roll forward*.

roll forward: the replacement of one call with a call that has the same striking price, but a later expiration date

Example: The call you wrote against your 100 shares of stock is near expiration and is in the money. To avoid or delay exercise, you cancel (buy) the original option and sell another one, with the same striking price but a later expiration date.

This technique is possible with single calls, although it is much easier to achieve if you have several hundred shares of stock. The more shares you have, the more flexibility you have in being able to increase outstanding option contracts as you roll forward, adding to your profits. Canceling a single call and replacing it with two or more options with later expirations is called *incremental return*. Your profit is increased as you increase the number of outstanding options on your stock.

One type of rolling technique is known as *roll down*.

incremental return: a technique of avoiding exercise when the value of the underlying stock is rising (One call position is closed at a loss, but replaced by two or more new call positions; the net effect of this is to produce a cash profit.)

Example: You originally purchased stock for $31 per share and later sold a call with a striking price of $35. The stock has declined in value, and you cancel (buy) the call position. You then sell another call with a striking price of 30.

A second rolling technique is known as *roll up*.

Example: You originally purchased stock for $31 per share and later sold a call with a striking price of $35. The stock is now worth $39. You cancel (buy) the first call, accepting a loss, and offset that loss by selling another call with a striking price of 40.

roll down: the replacement of one call with another that has a lower striking price

roll up: the replacement of one call with a call that has a higher striking price

In using the rolling technique, you can exchange an existing call for one that has not only a later expiration date but also a higher striking price. See Figure 5.4.

Example: You own 800 shares of stock that originally cost $30 per share (total cost, $24,000). You expect the value to rise, but also want to write covered calls. So, on March 15 you sell two June 30 contracts for a premium of 5, and receive $1000.

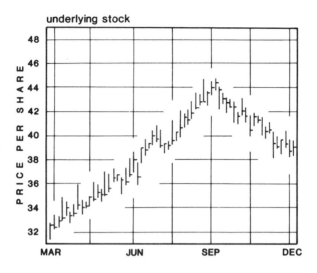

DATE	DESCRIPTION	RECEIVED	PAID
Mar 15	sell 2 Jun 30 calls at 5	$1000	
Jun 11	buy 2 Jun 30 calls at 8		$1600
	sell 5 Sep 35 calls at 6	$3000	
Sep 8	buy 5 Sep 35 calls at 9		$4500
	sell 8 Dec 40 calls at 6	$4800	
Dec 22	Dec 40 calls expire worthless	–	–
	totals	$8800	$6100
	profit	$2700	

Figure 5.4.   Using the rolling technique to avoid exercise.

On June 11, the stock is worth $38 per share, and you know your calls will be exercised. To avoid this, you place a closing purchase transaction to buy your two calls and pay a premium of 8 (total cost, $1600). You replace these canceled calls with five September 35 calls and receive a premium of 6 each (total received, $3000).

On September 8, the stock has again risen and is now valued at $44 per share. You again want to avoid exercise, so you cancel (buy) your five open calls and pay a premium of 9 (total cost, $4500). You replace these with eight December 40 calls and receive a premium of 6 on each (total received, $4800).

By December 22, the day of expiration, the stock has declined in value to $39 per share. Your eight outstanding option contracts expire worthless.

The total profit on this series of transactions is $2700. In addition, you still hold 800 shares of stock now valued at $39 per share, which represents an additional profit of $7200 should you decide to sell.

This incremental return combining roll up and roll forward techniques demonstrates how exercise can be avoided and profits ensured. Of course, the example is an ideal situation. The stock continued to climb but finally closed just below the latest striking price. You cannot depend on this pattern to occur with any consistency. But avoiding exercise is a practical and realistic approach to management of covered calls when the underlying stock's price is rising.

Stock

Sell 800 shares at $39 per share	$31,200
Original cost	24,000
Profit on stock	$ 7,200

Options

Sell 2 June contracts	+1,000
Buy 2 June contracts	−1,600
Sell 5 September contracts	+3,000
Buy 5 September contracts	−4,500
Sell 8 December contracts	+4,800
Profit on options	$ 3,300
Total Profit	$10,500

Whenever you roll forward, you benefit from higher time value: The longer until expiration, the higher is your income. But you also extend the period of time you are locked into the striking price. So for the benefit of extension, you also lengthen the period of risk.

There is an unlimited number of strategies you can employ to put off or escape exercise. The purpose might be simply to avoid having stock called away, or it might be to increase future income by avoiding an undesirable striking price level when stock is currently valued much higher.

Example: You own 200 shares of stock that you originally purchased at $40 per share. You have an open June 40 call that you sold for 3. The stock is now worth $45 per share, and you would like to avoid being exercised at $40. Table 5.2 shows the current values of options available on your stock. A review of this data reveals several rolling opportunities.

To begin, you will have to make a closing purchase transaction to buy your June 40 option at 6, accepting a $300 loss on that option. To offset this loss, you can use one of the following strategies.

1. *Strategy 1: Rolling Up and Forward.* Sell one December 45 call at 5, producing a net cash increase of $200 ($500 on the December call, less the loss of $300 on the June call).

2. *Strategy 2: Rolling with Incremental Return.* Sell two September 45 calls and receive $400, producing a net cash increase of $100 ($400 on the September calls, less the loss of $300 on the June call).

3. *Strategy 3: Rolling Forward Only.* Sell one September 40 call at 8, producing a net cash increase

Table 5.2. Current Call Option Values

Striking Price	Expiration Month		
	June	Sept.	Dec.
35	11	13	15
40	6	8	10
45	1	2	5

of $500 ($800 for the September call, less the loss of $300 on the June call).

If the underlying stock is fairly stable and moves up and down within a range of 5 points, it is possible to sell calls in an indefinite series, thereby canceling the open positions when time values go out of the premiums. Rolling techniques can then be used when the underlying stock's value moves above or below the typical range.

To show how this strategy works, Table 5.3 gives an actual example of trades over a period of 2½ years. The investor owned 400 shares of stock and traded with a discount broker. The sale and purchase prices show the actual cash transacted, including commissions charged, and rounded to the nearest dollar. The total net profit of $2628 occurred after 40 trades (20 buy orders and 20 sell orders). Total commission costs came to $722, so actual gross profits were $3350 and the investor realized a net of $2628 after the brokerage firm took its share.

The summary in Table 5.3 reveals examples of each type of rolling trade, plus an effective use of the incremental return technique. The investor was willing to increase the outstanding covered calls on as many as 400 shares of stock in order to avoid

Table 5.3. Selling Calls with Rolling Techniques

Calls Traded	Type	Sold Date	Sold Amount	Bought Date	Bought Amount	Profit	Notes
1	Jul 35	3/20	$ 328	4/30	$ 221	$ 107	
1	Oct 35	6/27	235	10/8	78	157	
1	Apr 35	1/15	247	4/14	434	−187	
1	Oct 35	4/14	604	6/24	228	376	1
1	Oct 35	7/31	353	9/12	971	−618	
2	Jan 45	9/12	915	12/16	172	743	2
2	Apr 45	12/16	379	2/24	184	195	
4	Jul 40	3/9	1357	5/26	385	972	3
4	Oct 40	6/5	1553	7/22	1036	517	
4	Jan 40	8/5	1504	9/15	138	366	
		Totals	$7475		$4847	$2628	

1. A roll forward: The loss on the April 35 call was acceptable to avoid exercise, since the October 35 was profitable.
2. A combination roll forward and roll up: The loss on the October 35 call was acceptable to avoid exercise at a low striking price. The number of calls was incrementally increased from one to two.
3. A roll down combined with an incremental return: The number of calls changed from two to four, and the striking price of 45 was replaced with one for 40.

exercise when current market value was greater than striking price. And when the stock's price was lower, the investor rolled down, but did not write calls below the original, acceptable striking price of 35.

Any form of covered call writing must be planned ahead of time. Besides the attributes of the option itself, the quality of the underlying stock must be taken into account. If you purchase shares primarily to write calls, chances are you will pick issues that are more volatile than average, as these often have more attractive, higher time values than more conservative stocks.

Whether you intend to write uncovered or covered calls, you will not succeed if you buy overpriced stocks that later fall far below your original cost. An example of an uncovered call write, with defined profit and loss zones, is shown in Figure 5.5. In this example, you sell one May 40 call for 2 (+ $200). This strategy of selling uncovered options exposes you to unlimited risk. If the stock rises above the striking price beyond the amount of premium received, exercise will create a loss. The stock could rise indefinitely. Upon exercise, you will be expected to deliver 100 shares at the striking price of $40 per share, regardless of current market value.

An example of a covered call write, with defined profit and loss zones, is shown in Figure 5.6.

In this example, you own 100 shares of stock that originally cost $38 per share. You now decide to sell one May 40 call for 2 (+ $200). This strategy discounts the basis in stock to $36 (purchase price of $38, less $200 received for selling the call). As long as the stock's value is at or below the striking price, the call will expire worthless. If it is above that level, the option will be exercised and your 100

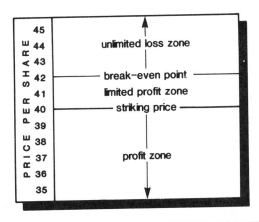

Figure 5.5. Example of uncovered call write.

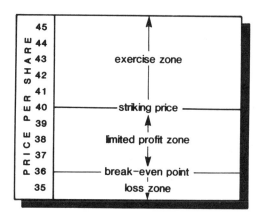

Figure 5.6. Example of covered call write.

shares will be called away. In that case, your total profit will be $400, consisting of 2 points in stock appreciation and 2 points for the option sold. However, selling covered calls also locks in the striking price. In the event of a substantial price increase, profits are limited to $40 per share.

As a call writer, stock selection is critically important to you. The next chapter explains methods for picking stocks with a call-writing strategy in mind.

CHAPTER 6

Choosing the Right Stock

C areful, well-researched selection is the key to good investing. This is true for all products and strategies. An investor whose stock portfolio is not performing well might be tempted to augment lackluster profits by becoming involved with options. However, the best chances for success as an options investor come from establishing a policy for selection of sound stock investments; fitting a suitable options strategy to that selection; and then following policies designed to maximize profits within a profile of acceptable risks.

Once your investment policy has been established, you need to stay with it. A portfolio of excellent stocks represents a long-term, worthwhile investment. It also offers opportunities for short-term profits in the options market. As a basic rule of thumb, select stocks you would like to hold for many years—whether you intend to write options or not.

One common error made by options investors is buying stock specifically because the current option premium is attractive. For example, a call writer might buy 100 shares of stock just to provide cover for writing an option. If this is done without qualifying the stock separately, it could spell trouble. Because of their volatility, some of the more volatile

stock investments also have some of the more interesting option premiums and movements. You need
to ensure that your personal risk standards are re-
membered and given high priority. While some option strategies can be highly profitable when the
stock's price falls, you also need to look to the
longer term and ensure the safety of your capital.

One of the great advantages to covered call
writing is that a minimum profit level is ensured.
This is a great opportunity so long as you also remember that stock selection is of critical importance. To show how the minimum profit level
works, consider this example.

Example: You purchased 100 shares of stock at a
cost of $38 per share. Your reason for buying this
particular stock was independent of any options
considerations. Now, several months later, you are
considering selling a call covered by the 100 shares.
One call expires in three months with a striking
price of $40, and offers a premium of 4 ($400). During that period, you would also earn a dividend on
the stock of $60. Your calculations assure you an
annualized profit of 48.4 percent (if the call expires
worthless) or 69.9 percent (if the call is exercised).

If the Call Expires

Call premium	$ 400
Plus dividends	60
Total profit	$ 460
Basis in stock	$3800

Yield if the Option Expires

(460 ÷ $3800)   12.1%

Annualized Return Earned in Three Months

(12.1% × 4)   48.4%

If the Call Is Exercised

Call premium	$ 400
Plus dividends	60
Plus capital gain	200
Total profit	$ 660
Basis in stock	$3800

Yield if the Option Is Exercised

($660 ÷ $3800)   17.4%

Annualized Return Earned in Three Months

(17.4% × 4)   69.6%

Note that the annualized return is computed by reflecting yield as if earned in twelve months. So when it takes only three months, the yield percentage is multiplied by four.

DEVELOPING A PRACTICAL APPROACH

Earning a consistently high yield writing calls is not always possible, even for covered call writers. You might be able to sell a call today that is rich in time value, and profit from the combination of capital gains, dividends, and call premium. But the opportunity depends on a combination of factors.

1. The price of the underlying stock is at the right price in two respects: first, in relation to the price you paid for the stock, and second, in relation to the call you want to write.

Example: You bought 100 shares of stock at $43 per share and would like to write a call with a striking price of $45. If exercised, you would earn a profit of $200 on the stock, plus the option premium and any dividends. So long as the premium is high enough to justify the position, it will be a worth-while decision.

2. The volume of investor interest in the stock and options is high enough to make those calls rich in time value.

Example: The stock you recently purchased has had exceptionally high volume lately because it is rumored as a takeover candidate. For the same reasons, the call premiums on the underlying stock are very rich with time value, the best possible situation for call writing.

3. The time until expiration of the option fits well with your personal goals.

Example: You would like to sell your stock in four months and use the proceeds to pay off a loan. You are confident that the stock's value will hold up, but in the meantime, you would like to augment your profits by writing a call. Because you will need your stock proceeds in four months, it makes sense to write calls that will expire before that deadline.

These circumstances might not repeat later. Writing calls requires patience and timing, and you will sometimes have to wait until the yield from writing a call will be just right.

In considering a covered call strategy, a common mistake is to assume that today's circumstances will be there in the future. For example, you might earn 48 percent on your first transaction. But you probably will not be able to consistently earn 48 percent. The ideal write will occur in the following circumstances.

1. The striking price of the option is higher than your basis in the underlying stock. In this case, exercise would produce an automatic profit in the stock *and* in the option. If the striking price is lower than your stock basis, exercise would produce a loss in the stock.

2. The call is in the money. This means it contains some intrinsic value, so that stock movement will most likely be paralleled with option value movement as well. While being in the money increases the risk of exercise, it also means a higher current option premium.

3. There is enough time remaining until expiration such that the majority of premium consists of time value. Even if there is little or no movement in the stock, time value will evaporate by expiration, the major point favoring the option writer.

4. Expiration will occur in six months or less, meaning you will not be locked into the position for an extremely long time. For some, even six months may be too long a period. However, the point here is that you don't want to assume that circumstances will remain unchanged indefinitely. The investing mood could be extremely different in a few months.

Example: One investor owns 100 shares of a stock that cost $53 per share. The stock is now valued at $57 per share. One call with a striking price of 55 expires in five months and has a current premium of 6 ($600). All of the ideal circumstances exist: The striking price is 2 points higher than the stock's original cost; the call is in the money by 2 points; two-thirds of the total premium is time value; and expiration will occur in five months. The investor will earn a substantial return whether the call expires worthless or is exercised. And if the high time value disappears from the premium, the short position can be closed at a profit.

This example illustrates a practical and methodical approach to writing covered calls. For the 6 points received from selling the call, the investor also gains 6 points of downside protection. So the net basis in stock is $47 per share (original cost of $53, less 6 points for the call). Even if the stock falls to that level, no money will have been lost.

SELECTING STOCKS FOR CALL WRITING

Some investors choose stocks based only on the potential for yield from covered call writing. This approach is a mistake if other criteria are not applied, because the best-yielding calls often are available on the most volatile stocks. So if you apply the criterion of call writing yield as the sole reason for picking one stock over another, you also increase the chances of wide price swings in your portfolio.

Example: One investor decides to buy stock based on the relationship of current call premium to the price of stock. He has only $4000 to invest, so he reviews only those stocks selling for $40 per share or less. His objective is to buy stock on which the call premium is no less than 10 percent of current value when the call is out of the money or at the money. He prepares a chart:

Current Value	Call Premium
$36	$3
28	3½
25	1
39	4
27	1¾

He decides to buy the stock priced at $28 per share, because the call's value is 3½, for a yield of 12.5 percent.

There are several problems with this approach. Most significant is the fact that no distinction is made between stocks. The issue selected is not judged on its own merits, only on the relationship between price and call premium. And by limiting the selection to stocks below $40 per share, the possible market for covered call writing is severely restricted.

There is also a failure to consider the time until expiration. You will receive a higher premium when the expiration date is further away, but you also lock in the position for a greater period of time.

This approach also fails to judge calls in relation to their current price. Return is increased on the call if it is in the money, which also increases the chance for exercise.

The value of locking in 100 shares to a fixed striking price must always be judged in relationship to the number of months until expiration. For example, a 10 percent or higher yield might be attractive for calls with a three-to-six-month remaining life, but is less attractive when the call does not expire for eight months. Yield is not a constant; it depends on time as well.

Comparing yields between current call premium and stock price also ignores the equally important time factor, potential price appreciation in the stock, and dividend yield.

Covered call writing is a conservative strategy, assuming that you have first selected stocks for their own investment value—not just because covered call writing looks good today.

Benefiting from Price Appreciation

You will profit from covered call writing when the underlying stock's current value is above the price you paid for the stock. In this case, you protect your position against declines in price and also lock in a capital gain in the event of exercise.

Example: You purchased 100 shares of stock last year when the price was $27 per share. Today the stock is valued at $38.

In this case, you can afford to write in-the-money calls without risking a loss, or you can write out-of-the-money calls if justified by the amount of time value. Remembering that the original cost was $27 per share, you have four possible courses of action.

1. Write calls with a striking price of 25. This will yield you premiums including a full 13 points in intrinsic value. If the calls are exercised, you would lose 2 points (the original price, less the option's striking price), but you would keep all of the call premium. And in the event the stock falls several points, you would be able to cancel the position by buying the option. This would produce a net profit in the call.

Example: You sell a call with a striking price of 25. A few weeks later, the stock falls 6 points. You can now cancel the call and earn a profit of $600, which offsets the price decline.

2. Write calls with a striking price of 30. In this instance, the intrinsic value is 8 points, and you could apply the same strategy as above. However, because your position is not as deep in the money, the chances of early exercise are somewhat reduced.
3. Write calls with a striking price of 35. With only points in the money, the chances of exercise

are very low. And in the event of even a minimal decline in the market value of the stock, you could buy the call and earn a profit.

4. Write calls with striking prices of 40 or 45. These are out of the money, so the entire premium is time value. The amount of premium will be lower, but you offset that with two advantages. First, it will be easier to cancel the position at a profit, because time value will disappear even if the stock's market value doesn't rise above the striking price. Second, if the stock's market value does rise and the option is exercised, you will receive that much more in profit.

If you hold stock that has appreciated in value, you face a dilemma every stockholder must resolve. On the one hand, you are tempted to sell now and take your profits. On the other hand, if the trend is upward, you don't want to sell too soon.

In this situation, covered calls might be the best answer. You provide downside protection with the premium you receive and lock in a capital gain at an attractive price in the event of exercise.

Example: You purchased 100 shares of stock several years ago and paid $28 per share. Today, the stock's market value is $45 per share. You sell a call with a striking price of 45, which has four months until expiration, and receive a premium of 4 ($400). Because this is an at-the-money situation, the entire premium of 4 is time value. If the stock were to fall 4 points or less, today's market value is protected by the option premium you were paid. And if the price of the stock rises, you would consider the $45 per share a decent profit on your investment. Even in the event of exercise, you would consider this a successful return.

AVERAGING YOUR COST

You can increase your advantage as a call writer if you *average up*, when the price of the stock has risen since your purchase date. You originally bought 100 shares, and the price is now climbing. By buying another 100 shares each time the price increases, your average price will be somewhere in between, as shown in Table 6.1.

How does averaging up help you as a call writer? An investor who buys several hundred shares of stock must be concerned with the risk that prices will fall. So you can start out buying 600 shares today (hoping the price will rise), or you can buy 100 shares per month over a six-month period.

Example 1: An investor buys 600 shares on January 10 at $26 per share. If the price falls to $20, he will have lost $3600 in value. But if the price rises to $32 per share, he will gain $3600 in value.

Example 2: An investor buys 100 shares on the 10th of each month, beginning in January. The

Table 6.1. Averaging Up

Date	Shares Purchased	Price per Share	Average Price
January 10	100	$26	$26
February 10	100	28	27
March 10	100	30	28
April 10	100	30	28½
May 10	100	31	29
June 10	100	32	29½

price rises each month, and by June 10 her average cost is 29½ per share.

The investor in the second example has reduced risks by buying 100 shares per month. The average price is always less than current market value, but the amount at risk is built up gradually. See Figure 6.1.

The investor who averaged up can sell as many as six calls. Because the average basis is 29½ and current value is 32, the investor can sell a call with a striking price of 30 and win in two ways:

- When the average cost is lower than the striking price.
- When the call is 2 points in the money.

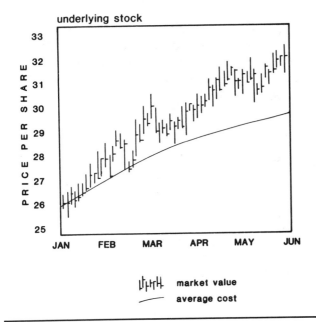

Figure 6.1.   **Example of averaging up.**

average down: a technique for absorbing paper losses on stock investments (By buying shares periodically, the average price is higher than current market value, but part of the paper loss is absorbed on average, thereby enabling covered call writers to profit even when the stock has declined in value.)

You also reduce risks and gain advantages as a call writer if you *average down* over time, as shown in Table 6.2.

The risk of buying stock today is that if the price falls, you cannot afford to sell calls. If your basis is higher than the current price, you must sell calls with striking prices below your cost so that, upon exercise, you will lose money on the stock trade. And if you sell higher striking price calls, the premium will be minimal. The solution is averaging down.

Example 1: An investor buys 600 shares of stock on July 10 when the price is $32 per share. If the price rises 8 points, he will earn a profit of $4800. But if it falls 8 points, he will lose $4800.

Example 2: An investor buys 100 shares of stock each month, starting on July 10. In July, the price per share is $32; by December, the price has fallen to only $24 per share. The average cost to the investor is $29 per share.

Table 6.2. Averaging Down

Date	Shares Purchased	Price per Share	Average Price
July 10	100	$32	$32
August 10	100	31	31½
September 10	100	30	31
October 10	100	30	30¾
November 10	100	27	30
December 10	100	24	29

The investor's average cost is always higher than current market value, but not as high as it would have been by buying 600 shares at the same time. See Figure 6.2.

With 600 shares, six calls can be written. The investor in the first example is at a disadvantage: His basis is $32 per share, and the current value is 8 points lower. He must write calls far out of the money, where premiums will be very small. To lock in 600 shares at a striking price of 30, for example, would not be worthwhile. If exercised, this investor would lose 2 points per share on the stock.

The investor in the second example has an average basis of 29. By writing calls with a striking price of 30, this investor will gain 1 point per share if the calls are exercised (before commission costs).

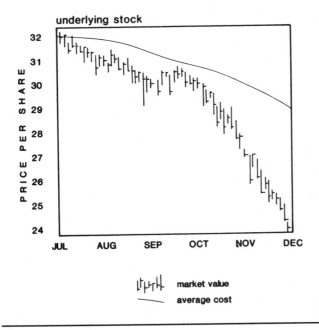

Figure 6.2.   **Example of averaging down.**

ANALYZING STOCKS

Stock should be selected based on fundamental or technical information, or on a combination of the two. It is a mistake to invest in stocks only for their potential as cover for writing calls.

Fundamental analysis provides you with methods for making financial judgments concerning the strength of companies and the value of their stock. Financial and economic factors, as well as management and company position within an industry, are the components of fundamental analysis. The fundamentalist studies the balance sheet and income statement, the history of dividend payments, economic prospects for the industry, and the company's competitive position. Also of interest is the quality and perception of management, the degree of change in management personnel in recent months and years, and relations between management and employees.

Technical analysis uses financial information only to the degree that it affects a trend. Technicians believe that trends provide the key for anticipating the future, that recent events dictate what will happen in the future. This belief is often applied to the actual price movement of stocks. Charts of recent price movements are studied for buy or sell signals. Some technicians depend on recent movements in composite indices or stock averages. Technicians also track buy and sell trends among insiders, or use market indicators of one kind or another to make their own decisions.

The value of either fundamental or technical analyses can be debated. A fundamental approach assumes that month-to-month price movement is completely random and that long-term value is best identified by an examination of a company's financial strength. The technical approach relies on the

fundamental analysis: the study of financial aspects of a company or industry to determine the safety and value of an investment (Fundamentalists believe that future value is determined by historical profits, dividend yield, the P/E ratio, and other financial trends.)

technical analysis: the study of trends and statistics in the market to identify buying and selling opportunities (Technicians believe that price movement is predictable based on historical patterns and trends.)

belief that the pattern of price movement enables an observer to predict the immediate future. By studying support and resistance levels, volume trends, and other statistics, market perceptions of value are anticipated, and decisions are based on interpretations.

Many successful investors, recognizing the value of both techniques, combine them to identify good values and to time their purchases and sales.

Call writers must not overlook the importance of tracking their stocks. There is a tendency to ignore the changing value of stocks held in a portfolio, because the call writer is preoccupied with other concerns: movement of stock price in relationship to the striking price, chances of exercise, opportunities to roll positions, and other matters related *just* to the status of the call.

The time will come when, as a call writer, you will want to close the call position and sell the stock. For example, you own 100 shares of a stock on which you have written a number of covered calls. But now, analysts say that industry's popularity is on the decline. You take this information as a sell signal and decide to pick a stock in an industry that has better prospects for future growth. To make a choice, you can apply both fundamental and technical tests.

Fundamental Tests

The successful call writer not only follows the value and status of calls, but also tracks the stocks on which the calls are written. Several fundamental guidelines should be followed to decide when to buy and when to sell.

The current price of a stock reflects the buying public's *perception* of value. This perception is affected by changes in the payment and rate of dividends and by the comparison of the current price in relation to earnings.

The price/earnings ratio (P/E ratio) is a popular indicator of perceived value. For example, one company earned $220 million in net profits last year and has 35 million shares of stock outstanding. That's $6.29 in earnings per share. The current market value of the stock is $35 per share. The P/E ratio is computed by dividing current market value by the earnings per share:

$$\$35 \div \$6.29 = 5.6$$

Another company earned $95 million and has 40 million shares outstanding, or $2.38 in earnings per share. The stock sells today for $28 per share. The P/E ratio is

$$\$28 \div \$2.38 = 11.8$$

As a general rule, a lower P/E ratio indicates lower risk. So the stock in the first example, with a P/E ratio of 5.6, should be a safer investment than the second one. But the P/E ratio is not always an accurate measurement of total risk. It should be looked at as part of a trend. If, for example, one stock had a P/E ratio last year of 15, and today it's down to 10, that indicates that the price today is more of a bargain than it was a year ago.

The P/E ratio, by itself, is an important fundamental test. But you should also consider several other fundamental factors.

- *Dividend yield*: dividends paid per share, divided by current price.
- *Profit margin*: profits divided by sales.

- *Profit on invested capital*: net profits divided by the amount of capital outstanding.

All of these fundamentals should be reviewed in comparison with past statistics, as part of an overall trend.

The P/E ratio should never be the only indicator you use to decide when to buy or sell. Fundamental analysis should be comprehensive, with a complete study of all the fundamental trends over a period of time.

Technical Tests

Combine fundamental stock tests with technical analysis to develop a well-rounded judgment of the stocks you hold or are considering buying.

One important technical indicator is the trend in volume. You can apply this information against the market as a whole or against a single stock. When volume increases, it indicates increased market interest in that stock. Increased interest can mean that more buyers want shares, but it can also mean that more investors want to sell their holdings. Growth in volume often accompanies significant price movement in either direction.

Chartists (those who track patterns of price movement) look for support levels—prices below which a stock is unlikely to fall; resistance levels—prices above which a stock is unlikely to rise; and breakout patterns—periods when stock prices exceed support or resistance levels. Predicting future price movement depends on tracking average prices over long periods of time and attempting to recognize chart patterns that foretell the direction prices will take.

Another technical indicator for stocks is the high and low price levels. Tracking this information tells you where today's price is in relation to the high and low range. For example, most detailed stock listings show the annual high and low. So when a stock has had a range between $26 and $45 per share, and its current value is $44, you know it's very near the high end of its range.

Some investors are comfortable buying only when stocks are in the middle of their range; others look at the overall pattern and buy stocks that show a pattern of growth over time.

No single fundamental or technical test should be used in isolation. The more information you use, the better are your chances of timing a smart decision. You can evaluate your stocks as part of a trend, combining both fundamental and technical analysis, by using a stock evaluation worksheet like the one shown in Figure 6.3. After filling in one line for each week or each month, you can look for trends in dividend rate and the P/E ratio (fundamental tests) as well as the high/low and closing price range (technical tests).

APPLYING ANALYSIS TO CALLS

To select stocks on which calls will be written, you need to identify an "acceptable" level of volatility and price change. Volatility is a technical test of a stock's price stability over a period of time. It is usually expressed as a percentage during a twelve-month period and is computed by dividing the annual low into the change in price range.

Example 1: You want to compute the volatility in a stock you are considering buying. Its annual price range has varied between $28 and $49 per share. Divide the difference between these by the low:

$$\frac{\$49 - \$28}{\$28} \times 100 = 75.0\%$$

stock name _____

DATE	DIVIDEND RATE	P/E RATIO	HIGH	LOW	CLOSE

Figure 6.3.   Stock evaluation worksheet.

Example 2: You apply the volatility test to another stock you are thinking of buying. Its price range during the last year was between $67 and $72. Volatility is

$$\frac{\$72 - \$67}{\$67} \times 100 = 7.5\%$$

The stock in the second example is much less volatile than the one in the first example. For a covered call writer, the smaller swing makes the second stock more predictable, thus more controllable, than one with greater volatility.

Fundamental and technical tests can be applied not only to identifying good values in underlying stocks, but also to the timing of selling covered calls.

A second test worth applying to stocks with covered calls in mind is the *beta*, which is a test of relative volatility—that is, price movement of a stock in relation to the market as a whole. A beta of 1 tells you the stock tends to move to the same degree and in the same direction as the whole market. A beta of 0 implies little or no reaction to market trends, and a beta of 2 is calculated for stocks that react most strongly to market trends or that overreact by moving further than the market average.

beta: *a measurement of the relative volatility of a stock, made by comparing the degree of price movement to movement in an overall index*

Example: Over the past year, the composite index—the overall value of the market—rose by approximately 7 percent. Your stock also rose by 7 percent, and its beta is 1. If your stock rose 14 percent, its beta would be 2.

As a general rule, more volatile stocks will also tend to have higher time value premiums in associated options. That is, time value will also decline at a sharper rate for more volatile stocks than it does for less volatile, more stable ones. The higher time value premium is an indication of the greater risks in buying stock and in writing options on those issues.

Because time value is usually high for a high-beta stock, premium value is also less predictable. It's possible to buy an option and see the expected price movement in the underlying stock—and still lose money. That's because time value can fall dramatically and in a short period of time.

Example: You buy one call for 5, with a striking price of 45 and three months until expiration, when the underlying stock has a current market value of $41 per share. Over the next two months, the stock rises to $47 per share, or 2 points in the money. But at that point, the call is valued at 4. The time value has declined 3 points, even though the stock rose by 6 points. The proximity of expiration has taken its effect.

Besides volatility and beta of the stock, covered call writers should follow the call's *delta*. The delta is a comparison of changes in an option's premium compared to the movement in the underlying stock. When the option premium and stock price change by the same number of points, the delta is 1.00. And when the premium changes to a greater or lesser degree, the delta reflects the change in the relationship.

Every change in the price of the underlying stock also affects the value of an option's premium. When an option is deep in the money, the delta approaches 1.00; thus the premium of that option will change by approximately 1 point in the same direction as price movement of the underlying stock.

When the option is at the money, the delta is usually about 0.80. On average, the premium will

delta: the relationship of change in an option's premium to changes in the price of the underlying stock (When the two move the same number of points, the delta is 1.00; a higher or lower delta can act as a signal to take advantage of adjustments in time value.)

change by $\frac{8}{10}$ of a point for every point of change in the value of the underlying stock.

When the option is out of the money, the delta becomes progressively lower. The further away from the striking price, the less responsive that option will be to price movement in the stock.

Example: You are tracking an in-the-money call. Its striking price is $35 and the underlying stock's current market value is $47 per share. You notice that each movement in the stock's price is paralleled by a corresponding change in the option's premium value. The only variance is evaporation of time value, if any.

Example: Another option you have been tracking is currently at the money. You have observed that as the underlying stock's price moves, it affects the premium value of this option about 80 percent.

Example: A third option is out of the money. The striking price is $65 but the stock's current market value is only $52 per share. Minor changes in the stock's market value have very little effect on the option's premium value. You notice that, as the option's striking price and the stock's current market value widen, there is less effect of price movement.

Being aware of the delta enables you to take advantage of conditions and improves your timing, either as a buyer or as a seller.

Open interest is another technical indicator that, like the delta, tells you something about the status of a particular option. It is a measurement of the number of option contracts that are currently outstanding. For example, the July 40 calls on a particu-

open interest: the number of open contracts on a particular option (Increases in open interest reflect the *total* contracts outstanding, but does not show whether volume is due to increased activity among buyers or sellers.)

lar stock have an open interest of 30,000 contracts today; last month, only 500 contracts were open. The open interest has increased significantly. Either buyers think the stock will rise in the future, or sellers believe it will fall.

Open interest by itself is of limited value, because you cannot identify whether the activity is created by call buyers or call sellers. But as the volume of open contracts increases, the trend tells you that other investors are active.

As expiration nears, you can expect open interest to decline. Open positions are canceled or rolled forward as the expiration deadline approaches. Sellers take advantage of a greatly diminished time value, and buyers take their profits. At the point of expiration, open interest always goes to zero.

Applying the Delta

The delta of a call option should be 1.00 whenever it is well into the money. As a general rule, the call will increase and decrease 1 point for each point of change in the stock's value.

In some cases, the option's delta will change unexpectedly. For example, an in-the-money call increases by 3 points when the stock goes up by only 2 points (a delta of 1.50). This growth in time value is a sign that investors perceive that option to be worth more than its previous price. See Figure 6.4.

Time value will not move in a predictable pattern, and it will vary from one underlying stock to another. So as the market perception of future value (both of the stock and the call) changes, time value will also change.

You can track the delta of a call to identify and time your covered write.

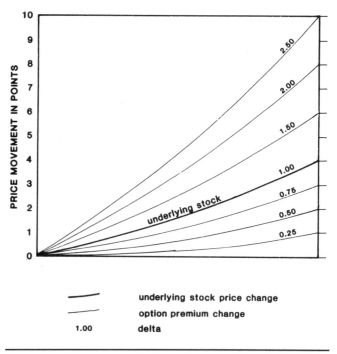

Figure 6.4. Changes in an option's delta.

Example: You purchased 100 shares of stock at $48 per share. During yesterday's market the stock rose from $51 to $53, based largely on rumors of higher profits than the analysts expected. The option with a striking price of $60 rose from 4 to 8, an increase of 4 points. The delta in this instance was 2.00: The stock rose two points, and the option's premium increased by twice that level, or 200 percent.

If a call's premium exceeds the movement in the stock, it can serve as a signal to sell a call. You can use the delta to track market perception and take advantage of distortions in time value.

The same strategy can be applied when you have an open covered call and are thinking of closing the position. For example, your call is in the money, and the stock falls 2 points. At the same time, the option's premium falls 3 points, a delta of 1.50. If this is a temporary distortion of time value, you will profit by entering a closing purchase transaction. There is obviously a shift in market perception, and that can serve as a signal that it's time to take action.

FOLLOWING YOUR OWN PERSPECTIVE

All analysis of stocks and calls is estimation. You cannot time your decisions perfectly, but must depend on a combination of fundamental and technical tests to give yourself an edge in the market. As a call writer, do not ignore the importance of studying stocks for more than today's call values. Buy stocks for the same reasons you would as a long-term investor and then use covered call writing as one strategy to increase yields.

Also recognize that covered call writing is a way to provide partial downside protection or to improve overall return on your investment. But writing calls is contrary to your objectives if you want to buy and hold stock for many years.

Example: You purchased 300 shares of stock last year as a long-term investment. You have no intention of selling these shares and, as you hoped, the stock's market value has been inching up consistently. Your broker is encouraging you to write calls against some or all of your stock, pointing out the potential for additional profits even if those calls were exercised. Remembering that your reason for buying the shares was long-term growth, you reject the broker's advice. Call writing would not be advisable, because it would go against your personal goals and market strategies.

You can certainly avoid exercise by rolling forward or up. But you might run into a situation where price increase is substantial enough so that exercise is unavoidable. Or a call might be exercised early. As a call writer, you must be willing to accept exercise as one possible consequence of your actions. You must be satisfied with the yield you earn in that case, and also with the requirement of actually giving up 100 shares for each call you write.

Do not overlook the importance of tracking stocks and evaluating them on their own merit. By preparing a performance chart like the one shown in Figure 6.5, you can track price movement by the week. A completed chart will help you identify and time a decision to sell or, if you hold onto the stock, the best possible time to write covered calls.

To succeed as a call writer, you must track the option and the stock. Making large percentage profits in calls is of no value if you end up with a portfolio whose current market value is far below your original cost.

Example: You bought 100 shares in each of four companies last year. Within the following months, you wrote covered calls in all four cases. Today, three out of four of those stocks have market values lower than your purchase price, even though the market is higher overall. You add up the total of call profits and dividends to discover that they are less than the paper loss on your overall portfolio. If you were to sell all 400 shares today, you would lose money.

stock _____ dates: _____ to _____

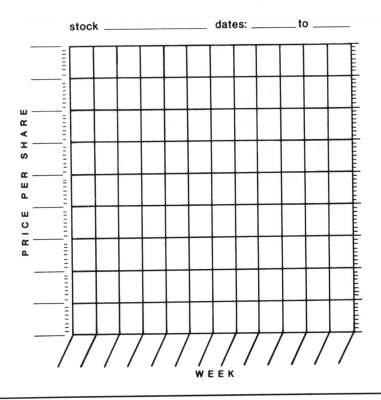

WEEK

Figure 6.5. Stock performance chart.

Certainly, this investor's losses would be greater if no calls had been written. The point is that without the covered call writing strategy in mind, would the investor have bought those stocks, or would others have been chosen? Relatively stable, safe stocks tend to have little time value in options compared to the richer time values in more volatile issues.

Perhaps the greatest risk of call writing is the tendency to buy stocks because calls are attractive bargains. A call writer has the best chance for success if the strategy is secondary. First, pick stocks based on thorough analysis and comparison. Listen to good advice or follow your own instincts, based on your own acceptable level of risk. Be a smart stock investor. Second, time the decision to sell calls on stocks you already own, preferably at a point when current market value is higher than both the striking price of the call and your original cost.

The next chapter explains how selling puts can be used for a variety of goals, including protection of long positions.

CHAPTER 7

Selling Puts

In Chapter 5, the special risks of selling calls were examined in depth. Every call seller has to recognize the fact that the underlying stock could rise in value indefinitely. The uncovered call seller faces an unknown degree of risk.

Selling puts is an entirely different matter. A put seller hopes the value of the underlying stock will rise. If that occurs, the value of the put diminishes and the seller realizes a profit. But what about the risk that the stock will fall? Because the lowest possible value is zero, the maximum degree of risk is easily identified and known in advance. Even a drastic decline in the underlying stock's market value can have only so much consequence. Even if the stock became completely worthless, the put seller's liability is limited.

Another way to look at the risk, perhaps more realistically, is to assume that the lowest practical level to which a stock will normally decline is its book value per share. Many popular stocks trade well above book value, so this might serve as a dependable floor for judging the risk of selling puts. You might assume that, even in the worst case, the stock's intrinsic value should never fall below book value. Thus, a stock currently selling at $50 per share that has a book value of $20 per share might be thought of as containing 30 points of risk (market value of $50 less book value of $20).

A put is an option to *sell* 100 shares of the underlying stock. So when you sell, or write, a put, you grant the buyer the right to sell 100 shares of that stock to you. In other words, for receiving the premium, you are willing to purchase 100 shares at the striking price, even if the stock's value falls far below that level. The risk, of course, is that the stock's market value will fall below striking price, and you will then have to acquire 100 shares—at a value above current market value.

As a put seller, you can reduce your exposure by selecting puts in a specific striking price range. For example, if you sell puts with striking prices of 50 or more, your maximum loss range will be 50 points, or $5000 per 100 shares. But if you sell puts with striking prices of 25 or below, the maximum loss range is never more than 25 points, or $2500.

EVALUATING STOCK VALUES

If you consider the striking price a fair value for the stock, selling a put achieves two things.

1. You receive immediate cash income from the premium for selling the put.
2. The premium discounts the price of the stock below striking price value.

If you are willing to purchase stock at the striking price, selling a put is a reasonable strategy. But the risk is that prices could fall far below that striking price. If the put is exercised, you will have to purchase shares above the market value at the time of exercise.

Buying shares above market value can be acceptable if you plan to hold stock as a long-term investment. You must be willing to take the paper loss—in the belief that the stock's value will ultimately rise above your price.

Example: You sold a put with a striking price of 55 and were paid a premium of 6 ($600). You considered $55 per share a respectable price for the stock. Before expiration, the stock's market value fell to $48 per share. The put was exercised at that moment. You were assigned 100 shares and paid $5500, which is 7 points above current market value.

Several points are worth mentioning in this example:

1. The outcome was acceptable as long as you believed that $55 per share is a good price for the stock. You would then believe that the current market value represents a temporary market decline. If your assumption is correct, the stock should eventually rebound.

2. The premium of $600 you received discounts your real basis in the stock to $49 per share (stock basis of $55, less option premium of $6 per share). So your true basis in the stock after exercise is only 1 point higher than current market value.

3. If the stock's market value had risen, you would have made a profit from selling the put. It would not have been exercised and would have expired worthless. In that outcome, the $600 would have been clear profit. Thus, selling puts in a rising market can produce profits for investors who are not willing to buy 100 shares.

Put sellers who seek only the income from premiums should select stocks with the best chances for rising in value. Fundamental and technical tests on stocks and the market in general should be applied when selecting underlying securities and their put options. If you do end up purchasing shares upon exercise of a put, you should make certain that you have selected stocks you *want* to own. Receiving income from premiums is only half of the total test. You must also sensibly evaluate the stocks on which those puts are written.

SETTING GOALS

There are four possible goals in selling puts: to produce income, to make use of idle cash deposits in a brokerage account, to eventually buy stocks, or to create a tax put.

Goal 1: Producing Income

The most popular reason for selling puts is to earn income from premiums. Time is on the side of the seller, so selecting puts with a large amount of time value increases the chances for profits.

Example: Last January, you sold a June 45 put and were paid a premium of 4 ($400). At that time, the underlying stock's market value was $46. Because market value was higher than the striking price, the entire premium represented time value.

If the stock remains at or above $45 per share, the option will eventually expire worthless. If, by exercise date, the stock is valued at between $41 and $45, the investor will make a limited profit. This range is the difference between the striking price and the premium received for the put.

A short position can be canceled by the writer at any time. But the option can be exercised by the buyer at any time, too. So whenever you sell a put, you must be willing to accept the stock at the striking price. For the income you receive from selling puts, you also accept the risk of having to buy 100 shares of stock above current market value.

A smart put seller is always aware of the potential profit and loss zones and will decide ahead of time when to cancel the position and when to keep it open. See Figure 7.1.

Example: You sold a put with a striking price of $60 and were paid a premium of 5 ($500). Your profit zone for this transaction is any price at or above the striking price. If the stock falls between $55 and $60 per share, it is in the limited profit zone ($55 per share is the break-even point because you received 5 points when you sold the put). If the

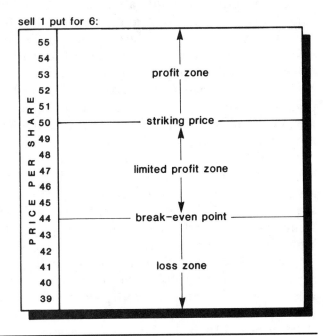

Figure 7.1. Put selling profit and loss zones.

price of the underlying stock falls below $55 per share, it's in the loss zone.

It is conceivable that a put writer could select stocks that will stay at or above the striking price and earn substantial profits over time. But the constant threat of exercise cannot be overlooked.

One of the greatest risks in selling puts is that you will end up with a significantly overpriced portfolio.

Example: You sold several puts over the last few months. This month, the market fell dramatically, and five separate puts were exercised at the same time. You have been assigned 500 shares in total. Now your capital is tied up and committed to shares you purchased well above current market value—even when taking into consideration the premiums you were paid. The only way your strategy can pay off now is to wait until the market values rebound above your net cost level.

The net cost level is the striking price, less the premium received for the put. You must also allow for commissions paid to a brokerage firm for buying and selling the stock and the option.

The risk of ending up with an overpriced portfolio is not limited to only a few points. It could be a substantial paper loss. If you sell a put with a striking price of 55 and the stock falls to $20 per share, you will end up owning stock 35 points higher than its current price.

You will be required to deposit cash with your brokerage firm to satisfy margin requirements. Whenever you assume a short position, the firm will require you to leave on deposit a portion of the striking price. Then, in the event of exercise, the brokerage firm is assured that you will be able to purchase 100 shares for each put sold.

Obviously, you must limit the number of puts you sell. You cannot exceed your capacity for buying stock at the combined striking prices of open positions.

Example: You have $12,000 to invest in the market today. Taking the traditional route, you could buy shares to the extent that you can afford. However, if you want to write puts, you will need to keep the $12,000 in reserve in case the puts are exercised. Based on that rule, you may never exceed 120 points in striking prices.

This limitation can consist of three options with striking prices of 40 each, of one option with a striking price of 120, or of any combination that does not exceed the maximum level. A broker might allow you to exceed the capacity of your cash balances. But if all your puts are exercised, you will then own stock on margin. Not only must you make up the difference between current value and your own net cost, you must also pay interest on your margin balance.

Whenever you sell puts, you accept the risk of exercise and cannot cover your position as you can with calls. A call write can be covered (when you own 100 shares) or uncovered. But you cannot cover a written put. A strategy called the covered put write consists of taking a short position in 100 shares of stock for every put sold. But unlike the covered call, your protection extends only the number of points equal to the amount received for the put. If the put's value rises above that level, the short put is not covered. So in practice, a put cannot be fully covered.

Put sellers must view their strategy differently from call sellers. With call writing, exercise is not necessarily a negative, since profits can be built into the strategy. But when a put is exercised, the stock is assigned at a value higher than current market value, without exception.

Put sellers can avoid exercise using the same techniques that call sellers use. Rolling forward provides greater time value and might delay or avoid exercise. However, avoid increasing the number of puts sold on one issue, unless you can afford to buy a greater number of shares and are willing to take that risk. It's a mistake to increase exposure just to attempt to avoid exercise.

Example: You sold a put two months ago and received a premium of 4 ($400). The stock recently declined below the striking price, and you would like to avoid exercise. The original put is now valued at 6 ($600). In order to forestall or avoid exercise, you close the original transaction by buying the put. This produces a loss of $200. At the same time, you sell two other puts that are currently valued at 4 each. This produces a premium of $800. While purchasing the original put cost you $600, opening two new positions yields $800 in new premium.

The problem with this technique for avoiding exercise is that risk is doubled. Now, instead of being at risk with one put, the investor has sold two in-the-money puts. If the stock continues to fall, he will be forced to buy 200 shares above current market value.

An alternative is to roll forward with a single put and reduce losses. The investor could have replaced the original position with only one put. Or he could have simply bought the put and accepted the $300 loss. The decision rests with how the stock is viewed at the time it has declined in value. Do you still consider it a bargain at the striking price? If so, exercise should be an acceptable event. If not, you should take the loss and keep your investment capital free for other uses.

You must also compare the potential loss in the put premium to the number of points difference in the stock. For example, the striking price is 45, and the stock has declined to $38 per share, which is 7 points below. If you close your put, you will lose $400.

In this case, a $400 loss is preferable to buying stock that is 7 points above current market value. Once free of the loss, you can sell another put and offset your loss in the first transaction with new premium income.

Goal 2: Using Idle Cash

When investors sell options, the brokerage firm will require a deposit of either cash or securities for at least a portion of the risk. With puts, the maximum risk is easily identified: It's the striking price of the put.

In some cases, investors keep their money on the sidelines, because they believe the stocks they want are overpriced. The dilemma is that if they're wrong and prices go higher, they are not putting their money to work. And if they're right, how long will it take for the market price to correct itself?

One way to deal with these unknown factors is by selling puts on the stocks already selected. You want to keep your money on the sidelines, fearing that prices are too high. By selling puts, you will make a profit if the prices go still higher, and you risk buying stock at the striking price if the stock's price goes lower.

Example: You are interested in buying stock as a long-term investment. However, you also believe that the market has risen too quickly and that a correction will probably occur in the near future. You also believe that the price of the stock you want is reasonably low right now. Your solution: Sell one put for every 100 shares you would like to buy instead of buying the stock. Place your capital on account with your broker as security for the short position. If the price of the stock does rise in the near future, the puts will lose value and can be bought for a lower price or allowed to expire worthless. In this way, you will benefit from a rise in market value without risking all your capital.

If the stock falls, you will be assigned 100 shares for each put you sold. But so long as that striking price represents a reasonable market value in your opinion, a decline in price should not be of great concern; you would expect the price to rebound in the future. The problem is only a temporary one.

Because the money is already in the brokerage account, the broker knows that the investor can afford to buy 100 shares, because money is there equal to or greater than the striking price.

Goal 3: Buying Stock

Another reason for selling puts is to intentionally seek exercise. Selling the put discounts the price by the amount of premium, and the investor is not concerned with price drops between now and the expiration date.

Example: You have been tracking a stock for several months, and have decided you are willing to purchase 100 shares at $40 per share. Current price, however, is $45 per share. You sell a November 45 put and receive a premium of 6 ($600). The effect of this transaction will depend on whether the stock's price rises or falls. If it rises, the put will become worthless and your $600 will be all profit. If the stock's price falls, the option will be exercised. When you subtract the option premium received from the striking price of $45 per share, your net cost will be $39—$1 per share below your target price.

In this case, the put is at the money, and the premium—all time value—is attractive. Even if the price falls far enough so that current value is below $40 per share, your long-term plans are not changed. If, though, the price of stock rises and the put expires worthless, you keep the $600 premium and can now adjust your goal. You can purchase stock at $46 per share or lower now that you've earned a $500 profit from selling the put. On a net basis, the stock will still cost you only $40 per share.

This process could be repeated indefinitely, so long as the put you sell expires worthless and the stock remains out of the money. Eventually, you will achieve exercise and buy the 100 shares of stock at what you consider an acceptable price.

Applying this idea, you do risk losing a buying opportunity. If the stock rises too far too quickly, you cannot make up the difference in premium income.

Example: You are interested in acquiring a stock at $40 per share. However, current market value is $45 per share. You sell a put with a striking price of $45 and are paid a premium of 6 ($600). You hoped the value would fall and that the option would be exercised, giving you ownership at a net cost of $39 per share. However, instead of falling, the stock's market value rose 14 points.

Your put expires worthless and the $600 you received is profit. But if you had bought 100 shares instead of selling a put, you would have earned $1400 in profit.

To succeed as a put seller, you must be willing to risk losing money in two ways due to unexpected price movement in the stock.

1. If the price of the underlying stock rises beyond the amount you receive in premium, you miss the opportunity to make a profitable investment. You settle for the premium only. This situation is not entirely negative. You still have your capital as security for future put sales and could make up the loss by following a continuing selling strategy.

2. If the price of the underlying stock falls drastically, you will be forced to purchase 100 shares at a price far above current market value. It may take a lot of time to make up the difference. And your capital is tied up in that stock, preventing you from pursuing put writing strategies at the level you want.

While the risks of put selling are more limited than they are for uncovered call selling, you could lose profit opportunities in the event the stock moves more points than the premium you receive—in either direction.

tax put: a strategy involving the sale of stock at a loss—taken for tax purposes—and the sale of a put (The premium on the put eliminates the loss on sale of stock: If exercised, the investor buys back the stock at the striking price.)

Goal 4: Creating a Tax Put

A fourth reason to sell puts is to create an advantage for tax purposes, known as a *tax put*. However, before employing this strategy, you should first check with a professional tax adviser.

An investor who has a paper loss on stock (where current market value is lower than the original purchase price) sells that stock to create a realized loss. This loss is deducted on that year's tax return. At the same time, the investor sells a put on the same stock, and the premium received off-sets the amount of the loss.

One of three results is possible.

1. The stock's market value rises, and the option is allowed to expire worthless. In this case, the investor has escaped the loss situation, taken a tax writeoff on the stock, and reports a gain on the option premium in the following year.

2. The stock's value rises and the investor closes the position, buying the put at a lower price than it was sold for.

3. The stock falls below the striking price, and the investor is assigned the stock. In this case, the overall basis in the stock should be lower than the original cost.

It must be assumed that if the stock is currently lower than its original cost, the put will have a striking price that is also below that cost. So upon exercise, the investor not only keeps the premium; the basis in the stock is also lowered.

The advantage to a tax put is twofold. First, you take a tax loss on the stock in the year it is sold, deferring the gain on the option premium until the following year. And second, you profit from selling the put option, as shown in Figure 7.2, in the following ways.

1. The premium income received offsets the loss.

2. In the event of exercise, the true basis in the stock is reduced from the original cost to the striking price.

Example: You originally bought stock at $38 per share, and it is now valued at $34. You sell the stock and realize a $400 loss. At the same time, you sell a put with a striking price of 35 and receive a

DATE	ACTION	RECEIVED	PAID
Aug. 15	buy 100 shares at $50		$5000
Dec. 15	sell 100 shares at $47	$4700	
Dec. 15	sell 1 Feb 50 put at 6	600	
	total	$5300	$5000
	net cash	$ 300	

PRICE MOVEMENT	RESULT
stock rises above striking price	$300 profit
	put is bought at a profit
stock falls below striking price	put is exercised at $50, net cost $47 (with $300 profit from tax put)

Figure 7.2.   Example of tax put.

premium of 6. If exercised, the result of this strategy is, first, that your $400 loss in stock is more than offset by the $600 income in put premium. Your net adjusted basis is now $36 (original purchase of $38 per share, less the $200 net profit from the tax put). Second, when the put is exercised, you buy 100 shares of stock at the striking price of 35, which is only 1 point below your adjusted basis.

Put sellers enjoy an important advantage over call sellers. The risk is not unlimited by the potential for indefinite price increases. A stock can fall only to the point that it becomes worthless.

An example of a put write, with defined profit and loss zones, is shown in Figure 7.3. In this example, you sell one May 40 put for 3 (+$300). The outcome of this short position in puts will be profitable if the stock remains at or above the striking price. If, at expiration, the value is lower than $40 per share, you will have 100 shares put to you and will purchase them at the striking price. Put selling involves a limited form of risk. With uncovered calls, the price of stock could rise indefinitely. But it can fall only to zero. Because you receive $300 for selling the put, the break-even price is 3 points below the striking price.

The greatest risk a put seller undertakes is that stock will become worthless. In that event, the entire striking price value will be lost. This risk is virtually eliminated by selecting stocks of companies with a solid fundamental strength and reasonable long-term prospects.

As with all option strategies, the best stocks for a put writing strategy are those that tend to move

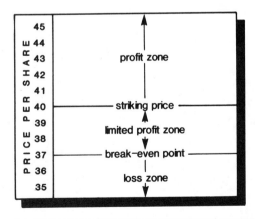

Figure 7.3.   Example of put write.

in a limited price range, thereby offering enough volatility to create short-term profits, but not enough so that there is great risk.

Put sellers must be willing to actually accept 100 shares that will be valued above current market value in the event of exercise. If the current price is reasonable in your point of view, and if you have thoroughly studied the company's strength and prospects for future growth, selling puts can be a smart way to increase income, discount the price of stocks you end up buying, and benefit from price increases without having to buy stock now.

In the next chapter, you will see how buying and selling strategies can be combined to increase income and reduce—or increase—risks.

CHAPTER 8

Combined Techniques

Option investors or speculators can employ only four basic strategies. These are: buying calls, selling calls, buying puts, and selling puts. As you have already seen, there are a number of variations on these four basic themes. Covered versus uncovered options, for example, represent vastly different levels of risk.

You also need to remember that the reasons for buying or selling options define the risk. In that respect, the utilization of an options strategy defines a completely separate investment. This chapter explains how the four basic strategies can be used in various combined forms. Long and short positions can be bought or sold together, or used to offset one another. Some combined strategies are designed to offer potential profits in the event an underlying stock moves in either direction. Other strategies can be used to minimize risk exposure while still offering the potential for profit.

There are three types of combined strategies: spreads, straddles, and hedges. A *spread* is the simultaneous opening of both long and short positions in options on the same underlying stock. The positions, in order to be called a spread, must have different striking prices or different expiration dates. Whenever the expiration dates are identical

spread: the simultaneous purchase and sale of options—on the same underlying stock—with different striking prices or expiration dates or both (The purpose is to increase the potential for profits, while reducing risks if the underlying stock's movement exceeds what is anticipated, or to take advantage of the timing of stock price movement.)

vertical spread: any bull or bear spread that involves options with different striking prices, but identical expiration dates

in a spread strategy, it is called a *vertical spread* or a *money spread*.

Example: You purchase a call with a 45 striking price and, at the same time, sell a call with a 40 striking price. Both options expire in February. This is a vertical spread.

money spread: another term for vertical spread

Example: You purchase a put with a 30 striking price and, at the same time, sell a put with a 35 striking price. Both options are scheduled to expire in December. This is also a vertical spread.

combination: any multiple purchase and/or sale of related securities whose terms are not identical

It is also possible to create spread positions by buying and selling options that vary by expiration date, or that represent a *combination* of different striking prices and expiration dates.

A *straddle* is the simultaneous purchase and sale of an equal number of calls and puts with identical terms. You will recall that terms include the same underlying stock, the same expiration date, and the same striking price. ("Terms" also includes type of option, whether put or call. In this application, of course, both puts and calls are included in a straddle.)

straddle: the simultaneous purchase and sale of the same number of calls and puts with identical striking prices and expiration dates

A *hedge* is the opening of two or more positions at the same time, all or part of which is done to reduce risks. For example, buying puts to protect your stock purchase against a decline in price is one form of hedging. The two positions involved are the purchase of stock, and the purchase of puts for insurance.

hedge: a strategy in which one position protects the other (Buying a put is a form of hedge to protect the value of 100 shares of the underlying stock.)

Most investors new to the options market will want to keep their strategies fairly simple at first. If you do venture beyond simple strategies, you are most likely to employ the vertical spread. Other, more advanced strategies are complex and beyond the scope and intention of this book. They are included here only to explain the entire range of possibilities in option trading. Considering the risks, commission costs, and complex analysis involved in advanced option strategies, they should be avoided by all but the most experienced investors.

Remember that what looks safe on paper might not always work out profitably. If you plan to use any of the advanced strategies—spreads, hedges, or straddles—you should first ensure that you fully understand all of the risks and costs of those moves, and that you have the knowledge and experience to proceed.

UNDERSTANDING VERTICAL SPREADS

Option investors use the spread to take advantage of the predictable course of changes in premium value. You can generally assume that when an option is in the money, its price will change more rapidly than when it is out of the money.

With this assumption in mind, you have an advantage when you open offsetting long and short positions. The position that is in the money will increase or decrease in price at a faster rate than the offsetting option.

Bull and Bear Spreads

There are two broad types of spreads: bull and bear. A *bull spread* provides the greatest profit potential if the underlying stock's value increases. And a *bear spread* will be most profitable if the stock's value falls.

In a bull spread, an option with a lower striking price is bought, and one with a higher striking price is sold. In a bear spread, the opposite is true. So there are four possible forms of spread: bull spreads using either calls or puts and bear spreads using either calls or puts.

bull spread: the purchase and sale of calls or puts that will create maximum profits when the value of the underlying security rises (Options with a lower striking price are bought, and an equal number of options with a higher striking price are sold.)

bear spread: the purchase and sale of calls or puts that will create maximum profits when the value of the underlying security falls (Options with a higher striking price are bought, and an equal number of options with a lower striking price are sold.)

Example: You decide to open a bull spread using calls. You sell one December 55 call and buy one December 50 call, as shown in Figure 8.1. At the time of this transaction, the underlying stock's market value is $49 per share. After you opened your spread, the stock's market price rose to $54 per share. When that occurred, the December 50 call increased in value point for point with the stock, since it was in the money. The short position call, at 55, didn't change in value by the same degree, as it was not yet in the money. Because of the advantage the spread created at this stock price level, it was the best time to sell.

A bull vertical spread will be profitable when the price of the underlying stock moves in the direction anticipated. That is, a bull spread involves buying the lower-priced option in the hope that the stock will increase in value between now and expiration. In that case, the long in-the-money option will increase in value at a faster rate than the higher, short option.

A detailed bull vertical spread, with defined profit and loss zones, is shown in Figure 8.2. In this example you sell one September 45 call for 2 (+ $200) and buy one September 40 call for 5 (− $500) at a net cost of $300. When the stock rises between $40 and $45 per share, the value of the September 40 call will increase dollar for dollar with the stock, while the short September 45 call will not rise in value as quickly. Up to the $45 per share level, the spread can be closed at a profit (assuming the difference in option values exceeds the cost of $300). Above the $45 per share level, the spread of 5 points in striking prices is offset by the long and short positions. Thus, maximum profits are limited and so are maximum losses.

A bull spread can also be entered using puts,

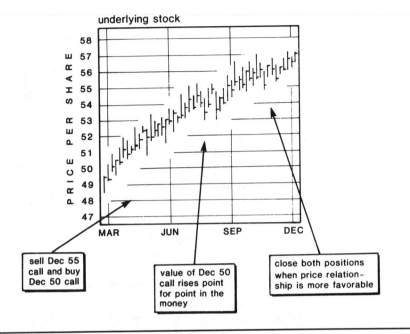

Figure 8.1. Example of bull spread.

in which case the in-the-money higher put will *lose* value more rapidly than the lower, long put.

Example: You enter into a bull spread using puts. You sell one November 45 put and buy one November 40 put. The stock's market value at the time of opening this position was $42 per share. Since the higher put, the November 45, is in the money, the premium value at the time of the transaction was greater than the lower, out-of-the-money put. If the stock's price later rises, your short position will lose its premium value at a faster rate than your long put. You would then be able to close the position at a profit.

A bear vertical spread will be most profitable

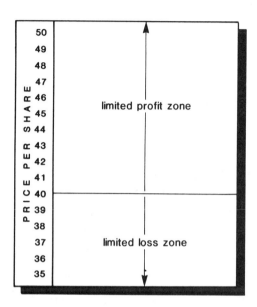

Figure 8.2.   Bull vertical spread profit and loss zones.

when the stock's value falls. In this spread, the higher-valued option is always bought, and the lower-valued one is sold. The spread can be entered using calls or puts.

Example 1: You open a bear spread using calls. You sell one March 40 call and buy one March 55 call. The stock's market value was $37 per share at the time. The premium value of the lower in-the-money call will decline point for point with declines in the stock's market price. If the stock's market value does fall, you will be able to close the position at a profit.

Example 2: You open a bear spread using puts. As shown in the example in Figure 8.3, you sell one

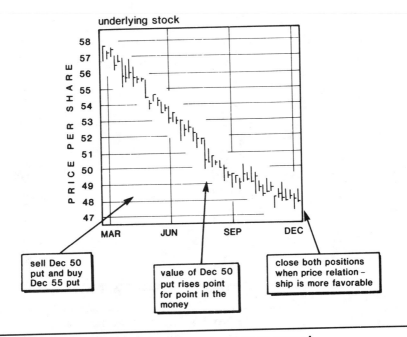

underlying stock

sell Dec 50 put and buy Dec 55 put

value of Dec 50 put rises point for point in the money

close both positions when price relation- ship is more favorable

Figure 8.3. Example of bear spread.

December 50 put and buy one December 55 put. The underlying stock's current value is $55 per share. As the price moves down, the value of your long put will increase point for point with the stock, while the short put will gain less. By the time the stock's value has declined to $51 per share, the position can be closed at a profit.

A detailed bear vertical spread, with defined profit and loss zones, is shown in Figure 8.4. In this example, you sell one September 40 call for 5 (+ $500) and buy one September 45 call for 2 (− $200), with net proceeds of $300. As the stock's value falls below $45 per share, the short call (at 40) will lose value point for point; the lower long call will not react to the same degree. As the $40 per

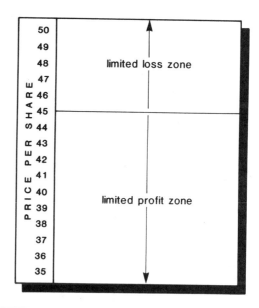

Figure 8.4.   Bear vertical spread profit and loss zones.

share level is approached, the spread can be closed for a profit. (Had this example employed puts, the higher in-the-money long put would have increased in value point for point with a decline in the stock's value.)

In this call example, the profit will be frozen once both calls are in the money—that is, when the underlying stock falls below $40 per share. At that point, the long and short positions offset each other, and the level of profit will be frozen.

In all of these examples, the risk is that the stock will move against the spread. You should close the spread before the short position gains value. However, if the underlying stock's value changes too quickly, you risk exercise or might have to close at a loss or reduced profit. In that event, your maximum risk is limited to the difference in the two striking prices, multiplied by the number of options involved. See Table 8.1.

Example: You open a spread by buying one option and selling another. The difference between striking prices is 5 points. Your maximum risk is $500 before brokerage fees, and assuming that both positions remain open.

Example: You open a spread by buying four options and selling four others. The difference between striking prices is 5 points. Your maximum risk before brokerage fees is $2000. The difference between striking prices is multiplied by the number of options.

Table 8.1. Spread Risk Table

Number of Options in Spread	Striking Price Interval	
	5 Points	10 Points
1	$ 500	$ 1,000
2	1,000	2,000
3	1,500	3,000
4	2,000	4,000
5	2,500	5,000
6	3,000	6,000
7	3,500	7,000
8	4,000	8,000
9	4,500	9,000
10	5,000	10,000

Box Spreads

You can open a bull spread and a bear spread at the same time by using options on the same underlying stock. In this case, your risk is still limited, whether the stock rises or falls in value. This strategy is called a *box spread*.

A box spread is the simultaneous opening of a bull spread and a bear spread on the same underlying security. A limited profit can be earned if the stock moves in either direction.

box spread: the opening of a bull spread and a bear spread at the same time and on the same underlying stock (The investor will maximize profits when the stock rises or falls in value.)

Example: As illustrated in Figure 8.5, you create a box spread by buying and selling the following positions.

1. *Bull spread:* Sell one September 40 put and buy one September 35 put.
2. *Bear spread:* Buy one September 45 call and sell one September 40 call.

If the price of the underlying stock moves significantly in either direction, portions of the box spread can be closed. Of course, this action will create an uncovered option. But if the stock's price then reverses, you can profit from price movements in both directions.

A detailed box spread, with defined profit and loss zones, is shown in Figure 8.6. The net proceeds from this box spread result from the following transactions.

1. *Bull:* Sell one September 45 put for 6 (+$600) and buy one September 40 put for 2 (−$200).
2. *Bear:* Sell one December 35 put for 1 (+$100) and buy one December 40 put for 4 (−$400).

If the stock rises between $40 and $45 per share, the bull spread can be closed at a profit. Above that

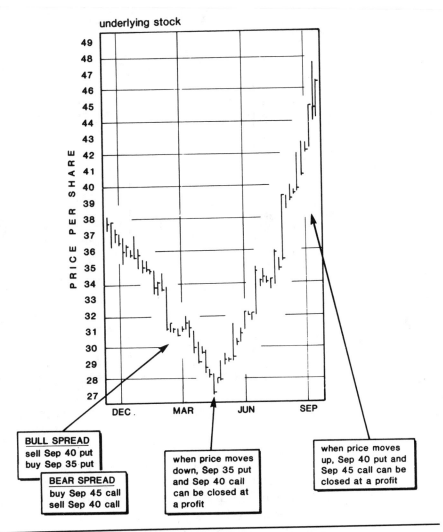

Figure 8.5.   Example of box spread.

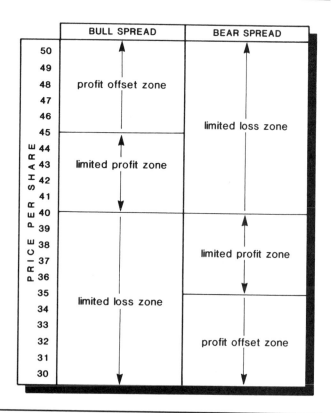

Figure 8.6. Box spread profit and loss zones.

level, the difference in bull spread values will move to the same degree in the money. If the stock falls between $45 and $40 per share, the bear spread can be closed at a profit. The in-the-money long position (December 40) will increase in value point for point with stock movement, and the spread values will close. Below the $35 per share level, the difference of 5 points in the striking prices will be offset.

Debit and Credit Spreads

The transaction of multiple long and short positions involves offsetting receipt and payment of premiums. And while it is always desirable to receive more money than is paid out, that will rarely be possible. A spread position is entered not only to create positive cash flow but to build the potential for profit while limiting the risk of loss.

A spread in which more cash is received than paid is called a *credit spread*, while the opposite is a *debit spread*.

UNDERSTANDING DIAGONAL AND HORIZONTAL SPREADS

In the previous section, examples were given of vertical spreads—that is, options entered with identical expiration dates but different striking prices. Beyond the vertical spread is a more complex form, which varies by time of expiration. Called *calendar spreads* or *time spreads*, these come in two broad types.

1. *Horizontal spread:* You use options that have the same striking price but different expiration dates.
2. *Diagonal spread:* You use options that have different striking prices *and* expiration dates.

Example: You enter into transactions that create a horizontal calendar spread. You sell one March 40 call and are paid 2 ($200), and you buy one June 40 call and pay 5 ($500). Your net cost is $300. There are two expiration periods involved with this spread. The earlier, short call expires in March, while the long call expires in June. This means your

credit spread: any spread in which the receipts from short positions exceed the cost of long positions (For example, a May 40 call is sold for a premium of 6 and a May 45 call is bought for a premium of 1, with a net credit of 5 ($500) before commissions.)

debit spread: any spread in which the receipts from short positions are less than the cost of long positions (For example, a June 55 call is sold for a premium of 2 and a June 50 call is bought for a premium of 6, with a net debit of 4 ($400).)

calendar spread: a strategy in which options bought and sold on the same underlying stock have different expiration dates

time spread: another term for calendar spread

horizontal spread: a calendar spread in which the offsetting options have the same striking price but different expiration dates

diagonal spread: a calendar spread in which the offsetting options have both different striking prices and different expiration dates

loss is limited in two ways: amount and time. This is illustrated in Figure 8.7. If, by the March expiration date, the first call expires worthless, the second phase goes into effect. With the short position eliminated, only the long position remains. If the stock then rises 3 points or more above the striking price, the long position can be sold at a profit.

Example: You create a diagonal calendar spread. You sell one March 40 call and are paid 2 ($200). You also buy one June 45 call and pay 3 ($300). Your net cost is $100. This transaction involves different striking prices *and* different expiration months. If the earlier-expiring short call is exercised, the later-expiring long call can be used to offset the assignment. Until the earlier call's expiration occurs, your risk is limited to the net cost of the two calls, or $100. After that, your break-even point is the higher striking price plus 1 point for each $100 of cost. In this case, the striking price is $45 and the net cost

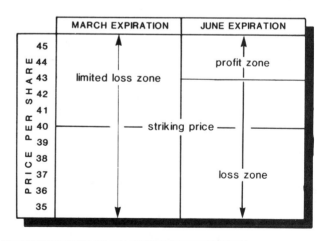

Figure 8.7. Profit and loss zones for an example of horizontal calendar spread.

is $100, so $46 per share is the break-even point. This is illustrated in Figure 8.8. Once the underlying stock's market value rises above this level, the June 45 call can be closed at a profit.

Giving different spread strategies the names vertical, horizontal, and diagonal helps to visualize what that means in terms of expiration dates and striking prices. This idea is illustrated in Figure 8.9.

A horizontal spread is a good idea when time value between two related options is temporarily distorted, or when a later option protects the risk involved with an earlier one.

Example: You enter into a horizontal spread using calls. You sell a March 40 call and are paid a pre-

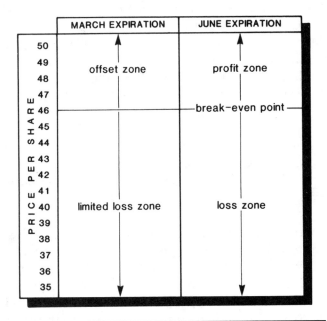

Figure 8.8.   Profit and loss zones for an example of diagonal calendar spread.

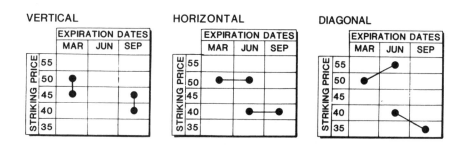

Figure 8.9.   **Comparison of spread strategies.**

mium of 4 ($400). You also buy a June 40 call and pay a premium of 6 ($600). Your net cost is $200. If the underlying stock rises, the long position protects you against the risk of the short position. Thus, maximum risk is the 2 points spent to enter the position. If the stock remains at or below the striking price between now and expiration, the March 40 short call will expire worthless. At that point, you would still own the June 40 call. If the underlying stock then rises above the striking price before expiration, you will be able to sell that call at a profit, or exercise it.

A horizontal spread can be useful in reducing existing risks when one option position is already open, and you open a second to protect that position.

Example: You sold a covered June 45 call last month. The stock's market value is currently above striking price. While you don't want to close the position, you are concerned that the call might be exercised. If that happens, you reason, you stand to lose future potential profits from growth in the stock's value. You decide to protect against this by buying a September 45 call, thus creating a horizontal spread. If the stock does continue to rise, your covered call will be exercised. However, you will be able to offset the assignment with your long call, sell that call at a profit, or repurchase the assigned stock at the striking price.

A diagonal spread is a combination of vertical and horizontal features. Long and short positions are opened with different striking prices and expiration dates.

Example: You create a diagonal spread. You sell a March 50 call and are paid 4 ($400). You also buy a June 55 call and pay 1 ($100). You receive $300 net, minus brokerage fees. If the stock falls, you will profit from the decline in value in the short position. But if the stock rises, the long position's value will rise as well. Your maximum risk is 5 points. But because you were paid $300, your real exposure is only 2 points (5 points, or $500, less $300 you received). If the earlier, short call expires worthless, you will still own the long call for the longer term and might profit from later price appreciation.

ALTERING SPREAD PATTERNS

The vertical, horizontal, and diagonal patterns of the typical spread can be employed to reduce risk. Going beyond this, spread techniques can be expanded through either the ratio or butterfly strategies.

Ratio Calendar Spread

The *ratio calendar spread* involves not only employing different numbers of options on either the long or short side but also varying the strategy by expiration month.

ratio calendar spread: a strategy in which the number of options bought is different from the number sold and in which the expiration dates of the options on each side differ (This strategy establishes two profit/loss zones, one of which disappears upon the earlier expiration.)

Example: You enter into a ratio calendar spread by selling four May 50 calls at 5 and buying two August 50 calls at 6. You receive a net of $800 before commissions. Between now and the May expiration, you depend on the underlying stock remaining at or below the striking price in order to profit. The break-even point is $54 per share.

If the stock is at $54 per share at the point of expiration, you will break even due to the ratio of 4 short calls to 2 long calls. Upon exercise, the two uncovered calls will cost $800, which is the same amount as the credit received when the position was opened. If the price of the stock is higher than $54 per share, the loss occurs at a 4 to 2 ratio. If the May expiration date passes without expiration, the four short positions are profitable, and you still own two August 50 calls.

The profit and loss zones in this example are shown in Figure 8.10. Note that no consideration is given to the following factors:

- Cost of commissions.
- Time value of longer-term premiums.
- Outcome in the event of an unexpected early exercise.

A complete ratio calendar spread strategy, with defined profit and loss zones, is illustrated in Figure 8.11. In this example, you sell five June 40 calls for 5 ($+$2500) and buy three September 40 calls for 7 ($-$2100), with net proceeds of $400. This ratio calendar spread strategy involves long and short positions and two expiration months. The short position risk is limited to the first expiration period, with losses partially hedged by the later long positions. As long as the stock does not rise above the striking price of the June 40 calls, the short side

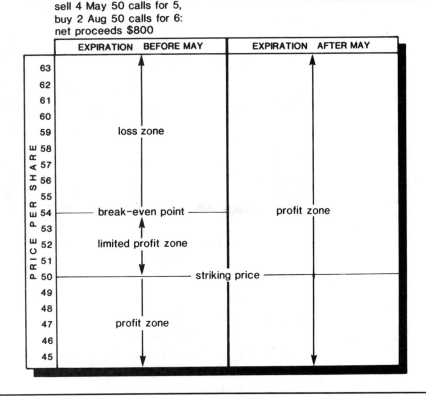

sell 4 May 50 calls for 5,
buy 2 Aug 50 calls for 6:
net proceeds $800

Figure 8.10.   Example of ratio calendar spread.

of the spread will expire worthless. However, you
have two uncovered options up until that point (net
of five short and two long calls).

Once the June expiration has passed, the $400
net received is profit, regardless of stock price
movement. However, if the stock rises above the
striking price, you will earn 3 points for every point
of increase in the money (with three long calls still
open).

Table 8.2 provides a summary of values for this
strategy at various stock prices as of expiration. If
the stock remains at or below the $40 per share

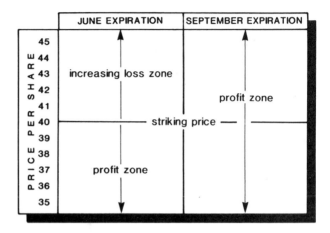

**Figure 8.11.   Ratio calendar spread profit
and loss zones.**

level, the proceeds of the ratio calendar spread are profit. However, the profit will never exceed this level. The loss, though, increases in the event of price increase in the underlying stock, by 2 points for every point of change.

Ratio Calendar Combination Spread

The ratio calendar spread strategy can be expanded into a ratio calendar combination, which adds the ratio approach to a box spread.

Example: As illustrated in Figure 8.12, you transact the following options.

- Buy one June 30 call at 3 (−$300).
- Sell two March 30 calls at 1¾ (+$350).
- Buy one September 25 put at ¾ (−$75).
- Sell two June 25 puts at ⅝ (+$125).

Table 8.2. Profits/Losses for Ratio Calendar Spread Example

Price	June 40	Sep. 40	Total
$50	− $5000	+ $3000	− $2000
49	− 4500	+ 2700	− 1800
48	− 4000	+ 2400	− 1600
47	− 3500	+ 2100	− 1400
46	− 3000	+ 1800	− 1200
45	− 2500	+ 1500	− 1000
44	− 2000	+ 1200	− 800
43	− 1500	+ 900	− 600
42	− 1000	+ 600	− 400
41	− 500	+ 300	− 200
40	+ 2500	− 2100	+ 400
39	+ 2500	− 2100	+ 400
38	+ 2500	− 2100	+ 400
lower	+ 2500	− 2100	+ 400

The total adds to net proceeds of $100, without figuring commissions. This complex combination involves 2 to 1 ratios between short and long positions on both sides (two short options for each long option). In the event of unfavorable price movements in either direction, you risk exercise. The ideal price change will enable you to close segments of the combination before expiration dates.

Considering commission costs, entering combinations with one or two options on either side is a costly strategy—especially considering the slim profit potential and wider risk of loss. That risk is somewhat reduced if shares of the underlying stock are owned. For example, when writing two calls and selling one, the risk of a price increase is elimi-

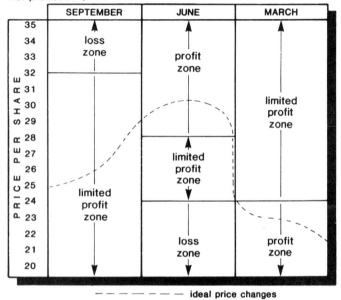

buy 1 Jun 30 call for 3 (–300)
sell 2 Mar 30 calls for 1¾ (+350)
buy 1 Sep 25 put for ¾ (– 75)
sell 2 Jun 25 puts for ⅝ (+125)
net proceeds $100

Figure 8.12. Example of ratio calendar combination.

ratio calendar combination spread: a strategy involving both a ratio between purchases and sales and a box spread (Long and short positions are opened in the same security but in varying numbers of contracts and with expiration dates extending over two or more periods in order to produce profits during periods of price increases or decreases in the underlying stock.)

nated because all call positions are protected. One call is covered by the 100 shares, and the other is offset by the long position.

A complete *ratio calendar combination spread*, with defined profit and loss zones, is shown in Figure 8.13. In this example, you conduct the following transactions.

- Buy one July 40 call for 6 (– $600).
- Sell two April 40 calls for 3 (+ $600).
- Buy one October 35 put for 1 (– $100).
- Sell two July 35 puts for 2 (+ $400).

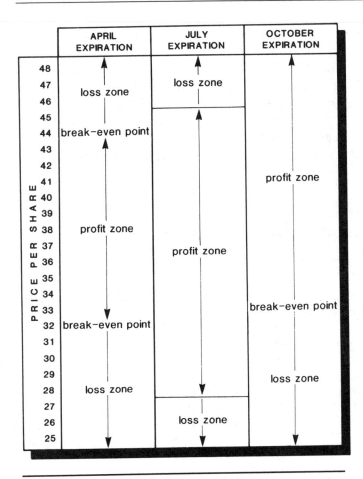

**Figure 8.13.   Ratio calendar combination spread
profit and loss zones.**

Your net proceeds are $300.

This ratio calendar combination consists of two
separate ratio calendar spreads. Profits can occur if
the stock moves in either direction, and maximum
losses are limited. There are three separate expiration dates involved. One danger of this strategy
is that, as earlier options expire, the later option

positions become more exposed to loss, and risk can increase. This situation can be reversed—so that the chance for later profits is made greater—if a combination is built using later long positions instead of short ones. Table 8.3 gives a breakdown of the profits or losses that will be produced at various prices as of expiration for the ratio calendar combination spread example in Figure 8.11.

Table 8.3. Profits/Losses for Ratio Calendar Combination Spread Example

Price	April 40 Call	July 40 Call	July 35 Put	Oct. 35 Put	Total
$47	+ $100	− $800	$ 0	+ $400	− $300
46	0	− 600	0	+ 400	− 200
45	− 100	− 400	0	+ 400	− 100
44	− 200	− 200	0	+ 400	0
43	− 300	0	0	+ 400	+ 100
42	− 400	+ 200	0	+ 400	+ 200
41	− 500	+ 400	0	+ 400	+ 300
40	− 600	+ 600	0	+ 400	+ 400
39	− 600	+ 600	0	+ 400	+ 400
38	− 600	+ 600	0	+ 400	+ 400
37	− 600	+ 600	0	+ 400	+ 400
36	− 600	+ 600	0	+ 400	+ 400
35	− 600	+ 600	0	+ 400	+ 400
34	− 600	+ 600	0	+ 200	+ 200
33	− 600	+ 600	+ 100	0	+ 100
32	− 600	+ 600	+ 200	− 200	0
31	− 600	+ 600	+ 300	− 400	− 100
30	− 600	+ 600	+ 400	− 600	− 200
29	− 600	+ 600	+ 500	− 800	− 300
28	− 600	+ 600	+ 500	− 1000	− 500
27	− 600	+ 600	+ 500	− 1200	− 700
26	− 600	+ 600	+ 500	− 1400	− 900

Butterfly Spreads

Another technique is the *butterfly spread*. This strategy involves offsetting options in a middle striking price range with opposite positions above and below.

It can be opened long or short, using either calls or puts. There are four possible versions of a butterfly spread.

1. Sell two middle-range calls and buy one call above and one call below.
2. Sell two middle-range puts and buy one put above and one put below.
3. Buy two middle-range calls and sell one call above and one call below.
4. Buy two middle-range puts and sell one put above and one put below.

butterfly spread: the opening of positions in one striking price range and offsetting them with transactions at higher and lower ranges (For example, two calls are sold while another is purchased with a higher striking price and another is purchased with a lower striking price. The buy/sell decision can be reversed, and the strategy can involve either calls or puts.)

Example: You sell two September 50 calls at 5, and receive a total premium of $1000. You also buy one September 55 call at 1 and one September 45 call at 7, paying out a total of $800. Your net proceeds are $200. This is a credit spread because you received more than you were paid. You will profit if the underlying stock declines in value. And no matter how high the stock's market price rises, the combined long positions' values will always exceed the values in the two short positions.

Butterfly spreads are often created when one position is later expanded by the addition of other calls or puts. It is very difficult to find opportunities to create a riskless combination, especially one that will yield a credit to you.

Example: You sold two calls last month, with striking prices of 40. The underlying stock's market value has declined to a point that the 35 calls are cheap, so you buy one to partially offset the risk of holding short calls. At the same time you buy a 45 call, which is far out of the money.

The cost of commissions makes it difficult to open a butterfly spread and still maintain a credit. And the potential gain must be evaluated versus both commission costs and the risk of exercise.

Butterfly spreads can be created with either calls or puts and with either a bull or bear structure. A bull butterfly spread would be most profitable if the underlying stock increased in value, and a bear spread would be most profitable if the stock's value declined.

A detailed butterfly spread, with defined profit and loss zones, is shown in Figure 8.14. In this example, you sell two June 40 calls at 6 (+ $1200), and you buy one June 30 call at 12 (− $1200) and one June 50 call at 3 (− $300) at a net cost of $300. This butterfly spread strategy will either yield a limited profit or result in a limited loss. It consists of offsetting a position at one striking price with a higher and a lower position.

As in many instances of the butterfly spread, the potential profit range is limited and too small to yield a profit after commissions. In this example, the potential profit and loss ranges involve three different exercise prices.

Table 8.4 gives a summary of profits and losses at different prices of the underlying stock (assuming point of exercise and no remaining time value). If the stock rises to $50 or more, the short positions are offset by an equal number of long positions. And if the stock declines, the maximum loss is $300, which is the cost of opening the butterfly spread.

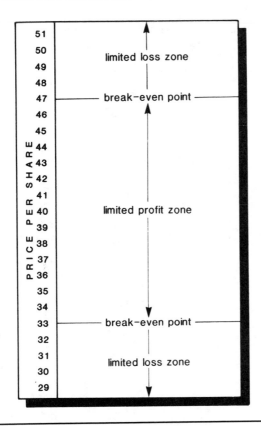

Figure 8.14.   Butterfly spread profit and loss zones.

UNDERSTANDING HEDGES

Whenever options are bought or sold as part of a strategy to protect another open position, the combined status is described as a hedge.

Long and Short Hedges

A *long hedge* protects you against price increases, while a *short hedge* is protection against price decreases.

long hedge: the purchase of options to protect a portfolio position in the event of a price increase, as a form of insurance (For example, an investor who is short 100 shares buys a call; if the stock's value rises, a corresponding rise in the call's premium will tend to offset losses.)

short hedge: the purchase of options to protect a portfolio position in the event of a price decrease, as a form of insurance (For example, an investor who is long 100 shares buys a put; if the stock declines in value, the increased value of the put will tend to offset losses.)

Table 8.4. Profits/Losses for Butterfly Spread Example

Price	June 50	June 40	June 30	Total
$51	+ $ 900	− $1000	+ $100	$ 0
50	+ 800	− 800	0	0
49	+ 700	− 600	− 300	− 200
48	+ 600	− 400	− 300	− 100
47	+ 500	− 200	− 300	0
46	+ 400	0	− 300	+ 100
45	+ 300	+ 200	− 300	+ 200
44	+ 200	+ 400	− 300	+ 300
43	+ 100	+ 600	− 300	+ 400
42	0	+ 800	− 300	+ 500
41	− 100	+ 1000	− 300	+ 600
40	− 200	+ 1200	− 300	+ 700
39	− 300	+ 1200	− 300	+ 600
38	− 400	+ 1200	− 300	+ 500
37	− 500	+ 1200	− 300	+ 400
36	− 600	+ 1200	− 300	+ 300
35	− 700	+ 1200	− 300	+ 200
34	− 800	+ 1200	− 300	+ 100
33	− 900	+ 1200	− 300	0
32	− 1000	+ 1200	− 300	− 100
31	− 1100	+ 1200	− 300	− 200
30	− 1200	+ 1200	− 300	− 300
29	− 1200	+ 1200	− 300	− 300
lower	− 1200	+ 1200	− 300	− 300

Example of a long hedge: An investor is short on 100 shares of stock. He buys one call to protect the position in the event the stock's price increases.

Example of a short hedge: An investor is concerned about the possibility that a stock's value will decline. To hedge against this danger, there are two possible courses of action: buying one put for each 100 shares or selling one call for each 100 shares.

Long hedges protect investors by covering their short positions in the event of a price increase; the original and hedged positions offset one another. Short hedges are the opposite. They protect investors against price decreases that will adversely affect long positions.

An expanded example of a long hedge, with defined profit and loss zones, is shown in Figure 8.15. In this example, you sell short 100 shares at $43 per share, and you buy one May 40 call for 2 (− $200). This long hedge strategy assumes that the underlying stock's price has declined since purchase—to the point that the combined time and intrinsic value of a call is available for a premium of 2. With this assumption, you accept a reduced total profit potential to eliminate completely the risk of loss. The loss is eliminated only until the expiration date of the call, while the short position in stock may be kept open beyond that date.

If the underlying stock increases in value, the profit potential is limited to the comparative advantage between the stock and call value; it will never

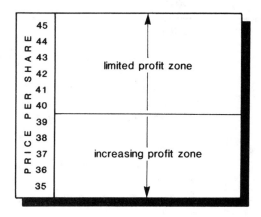

Figure 8.15. Long hedge profit and loss zones.

increase above that point spread. Increasing value in the short stock will be offset by the same degree in the long call. If the stock's value falls, the short stock position will be profitable, minus the 2 points paid for the call's protection.

Table 8.5 gives a summary of the position's value as of expiration at various prices of the underlying stock.

Reverse Hedges

Hedges can be modified to increase potential profits or minimize the risk of loss.

reverse hedge: an extension of a long or short hedge in which more options are purchased than needed to provide insurance (For example, an investor is short 200 shares, and buys three calls; if the price rises, every 2 points of loss on the short stock position will be offset by 3 points of gain in the calls.)

A *reverse hedge* involves protecting a stock position to a greater degree than required. For example, you are short 100 shares of stock. You buy two calls, thereby providing twice the protection needed and also giving yourself the potential for additional profits in the event the stock does rise.

An expanded example of a reverse hedge, with defined profit and loss zones, is shown in Figure

Table 8.5. Profits/Losses from the Long Hedge Example

Price	Stock	Call	Total
$45	− $200	+ $300	+ $100
44	100	+ 200	+ 100
43	0	+ 100	+ 100
42	+ 100	0	+ 100
41	+ 200	− 100	+ 100
40	+ 300	− 200	+ 100
39	+ 400	− 200	+ 200
38	+ 500	− 200	+ 300
37	+ 600	− 200	+ 400
36	+ 700	− 200	+ 500
35	+ 800	− 200	+ 600

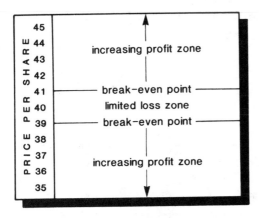

Figure 8.16. Reverse hedge profit and loss zones.

8.16. In this example, you sell short 100 shares at $43 per share, and you buy two May 40 calls at 2 (– $400). This reverse hedge strategy solves the problem faced by the investor who utilizes a long hedge. That is, the reverse hedge will produce profits if the stock's value increases or decreases by enough points to eliminate the cost of buying calls. In this example, 100 shares were sold short at $43 per share, and two May 40 calls were bought. (Like the previous example, it must be assumed that the stock's price has declined since the short sale, so that the option's cost is not prohibitive.)

In this case, the reverse hedge creates its advantage in two ways: First, it protects the short position in the event of a price increase; second, the extra call adds profit potential to the position. And if the stock falls, the short position's profit potential is reduced by the cost of the calls.

Table 8.6 gives a summary of the position's value as of expiration at various prices of the underlying stock.

Table 8.6. Profits/Losses from Reverse Hedge Example

Price	Stock	Call	Total
$45	− $200	+ $600	+ $400
44	100	+ 400	+ 300
43	0	+ 200	+ 200
42	+ 100	0	+ 100
41	+ 200	− 200	0
40	+ 300	− 400	− 100
39	+ 400	− 400	0
38	+ 500	− 400	+ 100
37	+ 600	− 400	+ 200
36	+ 700	− 400	+ 300
35	+ 800	− 400	+ 400

Variable Hedges

variable hedge: a hedge between two related option positions, where one side involves more options than the other (For example, you buy three calls and sell one at a lower striking price. The difference in premium reduces the cost and might even result in cash proceeds, but the potential loss from the short call is offset by potential gains in the long calls.)

Hedging can protect a long or short position in the underlying security, or it can reduce or eliminate risks in other option positions. Hedging is achieved with the various forms of spreads and combinations described in this chapter. And by varying the number of options on one side or the other, you create a *variable hedge*.

Example: You buy three May 60 calls and sell one May 55 call. If the price increases beyond the $60 per share level, your long position will increase by $3 for every $1 increase in the short position. If the stock falls, the short position can be closed at a profit.

Long and short variable hedge strategies with defined profit zones are illustrated in Figure 8.17. In the long variable hedge example, you buy three June 65 calls for 1 (− $300) and sell one June 60

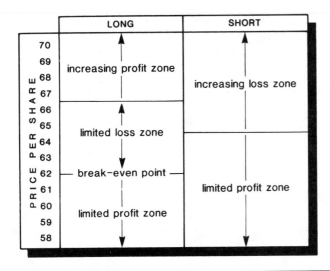

Figure 8.17.   Variable hedge profit and loss zones.

calls for 5 (+ $500), with net proceeds of $200. This long variable hedge strategy will achieve maximum profit if the underlying security rises in value. Above the striking price of $65 per share, the long calls will increase by $3 for each point in the stock, while the short position will offset only $1 per point. If the stock declines, all of the calls will lose value, and the proceeds of $200 will be profitable. Table 8.7 gives a summary of this position's value as of expiration, at different stock prices.

In the short variable hedge example in Figure 8.17, you sell five June 60 calls for 5 (+ $2500) and buy three June 65 calls for 1 (− $300), with net proceeds of $2200. This short variable hedge strategy is a more aggressive form of variable hedge, with a higher level of proceeds and a correspondingly higher risk. When the offsetting call positions are eliminated, two calls are uncovered. A decline in the underlying stock's value will result in the

Table 8.7. Profits/Losses from the Long Variable Hedge Example

Price	Stock	Call	Total
$70	+ $1200	− $500	+ $700
69	+ 900	− 400	+ 500
68	+ 600	− 300	+ 300
67	+ 300	− 200	+ 100
66	0	− 100	− 100
65	− 300	0	− 300
64	− 300	+ 100	− 200
63	− 300	+ 200	− 100
62	− 300	+ 300	0
61	− 300	+ 400	+ 100
60	− 300	+ 500	+ 200
59	− 300	+ 500	+ 200
58	− 300	+ 500	+ 200

entire $2200 being a profit. However, a rise in price will create an increasing level of losses. The outcomes of the short hedge at various stock prices as of expiration are given in Table 8.8.

Ratio Write

Another form of hedging is the *ratio write*. A covered call writer is said to be 100 percent covered when one call is sold for every 100 shares of stock. A ratio write exists when the relationship between calls and shares of stock is higher or lower than one to one. See Table 8.9.

Example: You presently own 75 shares of stock, and you sell a call. Because even a small portion of your total is uncovered, you actually have two separate positions: 75 shares of stock and one uncovered call. But if the call is exercised, your 75 shares will reduce the penalty involved. For practi-

ratio write: a relationship between long stock and short calls, other than one to one, that reduces risk on a portion of the total calls (For example, the owner of 400 shares sells five calls for a 5 to 4 ratio write involving four covered calls and one uncovered call, or 80 percent coverage of the entire position.)

Table 8.8.   Profits/Losses from the Short Variable Hedge Example

Price	Stock	Call	Total
$70	− $2500	+ $500	− $1300
69	− 2000	+ 400	− 1100
68	− 1500	+ 300	− 900
67	− 1000	+ 200	− 700
66	− 500	0	− 500
65	0	− 300	− 300
64	+ 500	− 300	+ 200
63	+ 1000	− 300	+ 700
62	+ 1500	− 300	+ 1200
61	+ 2000	− 300	+ 1700
60	+ 2500	− 300	+ 2200
59	+ 2500	− 300	+ 2200
58	+ 2500	− 300	+ 2200

cal purposes, your short position is 75 percent covered. The ratio write is 1 to ¾.

Example: You own 300 shares of an underlying stock and you recently sold 4 calls. This may be viewed as having three covered calls and one uncovered call; or it may be viewed as a 4 to 3 ratio write.

Table 8.9.   Ratio Writes

Calls Sold	Shares Owned	Percent Coverage	Ratio
1	75	75%	1 to ¾
2	150	75	2 to 1½
3	200	67	3 to 2
4	300	75	4 to 3
5	300	60	5 to 3
5	400	80	5 to 4

An expanded example of the ratio write, with defined profit and loss zones, is shown in Figure 8.18. In this example, you buy 50 shares of stock at $38, and you sell one September 40 call for 3 (+ $300). This ratio write strategy is a partially covered call. Half of the risk in the short position is offset by the 50 calls held long. If the value of the underlying

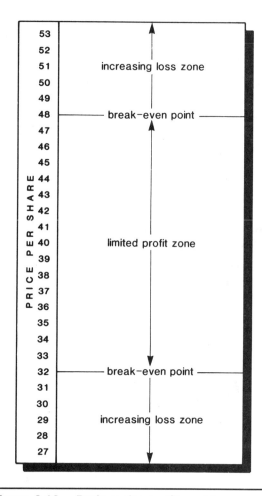

Figure 8.18. Ratio write profit and loss zones.

stock increases, the degree of risk is cut in half by the shares. However, if the stock's price falls far enough, a loss in the stock will offset the premium received by selling the call. A summary of the strategy, assuming various stock prices as of expiration, is given in Table 8.10.

UNDERSTANDING STRADDLES

While spreads involve buying and selling options with different terms, straddles are the simultane-

Table 8.10. Profits/Losses from the Ratio Write Example

Price	July 40 Call	July 40 Put	Total
$50	+ $600	− $700	− $100
49	+ 550	− 600	− 50
48	+ 500	− 500	0
47	+ 450	− 400	+ 50
46	+ 400	− 300	+ 100
45	+ 350	− 200	+ 150
44	+ 300	− 100	+ 200
43	+ 250	0	+ 250
42	+ 200	+ 100	+ 300
41	+ 150	+ 200	+ 350
40	+ 100	+ 300	+ 400
39	+ 50	+ 300	+ 350
38	0	+ 300	+ 300
37	− 50	+ 300	+ 250
36	− 100	+ 300	+ 200
35	− 150	+ 300	+ 150
34	− 200	+ 300	+ 100
33	− 250	+ 300	+ 50
32	− 300	+ 300	0
31	− 350	+ 300	− 50
30	− 400	+ 300	− 100

ous purchase and sale of options with the same striking price and expiration date.

Long Straddle

long straddle: the purchase of the same number of calls and puts with identical striking prices and expiration dates (This strategy will be profitable if the stock's price moves above or below the striking price to a degree greater than the total cost of buying options.)

A *long straddle* creates a middle loss zone and the potential for profit in the event of extreme price increases or decreases in the underlying stock.

Example: You enter into a long straddle. You buy one February 40 call and pay a premium of 2 ($200), and you also buy one February 40 put for a premium of 1 ($100). Your total cost is $300. If the underlying stock's market value remains within 3 points of the striking price, neither of these options can result in a profit. The 3 points in intrinsic value for either option offsets your net cost for the straddle. Once the stock's price is higher than the striking price by 3 points, or lower by 3 points, the long straddle will become profitable.

An example of a long straddle with defined profit and loss zones is illustrated in Figure 8.19. In this example, you buy one July 40 call for 3 (− $300) and one July 40 put for 1 (− $100) at a net cost of $400. This long straddle strategy involves assuming a long position in calls and puts of the same stock, with the same striking price and expiration date. It will become profitable if the underlying stock's price movement is substantial enough in either direction to exceed the cost of opening the position. Table 8.11 gives a summary of the outcomes at various stock prices as of expiration.

short straddle: the sale of the same number of calls and puts with identical striking prices and expiration dates (This strategy will be profitable if the stock's price does not move away from the striking price to a degree greater than the proceeds received by the investor.)

Short Straddle

A *short straddle* involves selling a call and a put with the same expiration date and striking price. This

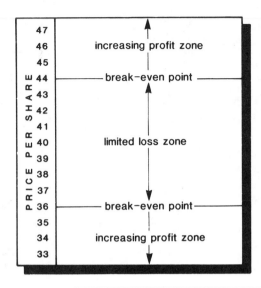

Figure 8.19.   Long straddle profit and loss zones.

action creates a middle ground for both potential profits as well as the risk of losses if the underlying stock exceeds that range on either side.

Example: You create a short straddle. You sell one March 50 call and receive 2; you also sell a March 50 put and receive 1. The total you receive is $300. So long as the underlying stock's price remains within 3 points from the striking price, any intrinsic value in either option offsets the premium you received. Once the underlying stock's price breaks out above or below the 3-point range, the short straddle will result in a loss.

The theory is fine on its own. However, this strategy does not take into account the costs involved with being exercised, which is likely in this case. One short position or the other will be in the money

Table 8.11. Profits/Losses from the Long Straddle Example

Price	July 40 Call	July 40 Put	Total
$47	+ $400	− $100	+ $300
46	+ 300	− 100	+ 200
45	+ 200	− 100	+ 100
44	+ 100	− 100	0
43	0	− 100	− 100
42	− 100	− 100	− 200
41	− 200	− 100	− 300
40	− 300	− 100	− 400
39	− 300	0	− 300
38	− 300	+ 100	− 200
37	− 300	+ 200	− 100
36	− 300	+ 300	0
35	− 300	+ 400	+ 100
34	− 300	+ 500	+ 200
33	− 300	+ 600	+ 300

at some time prior to expiration, unless the underlying stock remains steadily at the striking price for the entire term. Realistically, it is very likely that one of the options in your short straddle will be exercised. A thin margin of profit could be easily absorbed in brokerage fees. You might also end up having to buy or sell 100 shares of stock. The important question to ask: Is the risk worth the premium you will receive for a short straddle?

An example of the short straddle strategy, with defined profit and loss zones, is shown in Figure 8.20. In this example, you sell one July 40 call for 3 (+ $300) and one July 40 put for 1 (+ $100), with net proceeds of $400. This short straddle strategy is exactly opposite of the long straddle. In this case, the position consists of two short positions, one

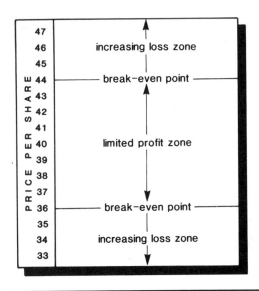

Figure 8.20.   Short straddle profit and loss zones.

each in the call and the put of the same underlying security with the same striking price and expiration date. So long as the underlying stock's value remains within a range above or below the striking price, a profit will result. In this example, that range is 4 points (proceeds of selling the options). Unless the expiration price is equal to the striking price, or the position is closed before expiration, either the call or the put will be exercised. Table 8.12 gives a summary of the short straddle's outcomes, given various stock prices as of expiration.

Actual profits and losses must be adjusted to allow for the cost of commissions upon opening and closing the straddle. The more money you have to spend to purchase options, the lower your chances for profit in the short straddle. And the less money you receive for selling short positions, the lower your profit potential. See Figure 8.21.

Table 8.12. Profits/Losses from the Short Straddle Example

Price	July 40 Call	July 40 Put	Total
$47	− $400	+ $100	− $300
46	− 300	+ 100	− 200
45	− 200	+ 100	− 100
44	− 100	+ 100	0
43	0	+ 100	+ 100
42	+ 100	+ 100	+ 200
41	+ 200	+ 100	+ 300
40	+ 300	+ 100	+ 400
39	+ 300	0	+ 300
38	+ 300	− 100	+ 200
37	+ 300	− 200	+ 100
36	+ 300	− 300	0
35	+ 300	− 400	− 100
34	+ 300	− 500	− 200
33	+ 300	− 600	− 300

USING COMBINED TECHNIQUES THEORY AND PRACTICE

Advanced option strategies expose you to danger, especially when short positions are involved. If you decide to attempt any of these ideas in your own portfolio, you should remember the following points.

1. Brokerage fees will reduce profit margins and extend potential loss zones in combined technique strategies. A marginal profit potential might be eliminated completely by the cost of doing business. This problem declines as the number of options increases; however, that also requires you to assume greater risks.

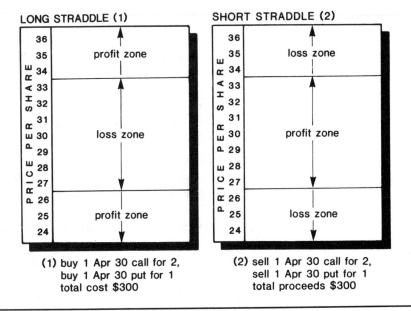

Figure 8.21. **Comparison of long and short straddle strategies.**

2. Buyers have the right to exercise their calls or puts at any time. It is easy to assume that exercise takes place only at the point of expiration. Never assume that this risk exists only at the end of the cycle. Be sure to evaluate your combined strategies with two questions in mind: First, are you willing to live with the risk of exercise for the part of your combined strategy that is short? And second, what happens to the balance of your combined strategy in the event that the short part of it is exercised?

3. All combined strategies should be evaluated with a realistic point of view. The potential reward should be thought of in relation to the risk.

4. You might be able to devise a series of interesting combined techniques. But remember that whenever you assume short positions, you will be limited. Your broker will require you to meet minimum margin requirements, meaning you will need to commit cash or securities in your brokerage account, for as long as the short positions exist.

5. Never employ a strategy until you fully understand all of the risks involved. You also need to identify the appropriate actions to take in the event of each possible outcome; then you need to take the appropriate action when each type of price movement does occur.

6. Option strategies can be worked out on paper, to the extent that you become convinced you can't fail. They might seem fairly simple and safe but, in practice, are more involved. Risk is something you need to experience before you can understand it completely. Only experience can demonstrate the differences between theory and practice in options trading. Sudden changes in the price of the underlying stock, in the market in general, or in the market demand for options all can and will affect profitability.

The next chapter explains why each investor needs to devise a personalized strategy. No one person will find any one approach universally right or comfortable.

CHAPTER 9

Choosing Your Own Strategy

Y ou will decide to include options in your portfolio if that is an appropriate and suitable strategy. And if your investor profile dictates that you should not be involved with options on any level, you should not pursue this idea.

Ultimately, your success as an investor depends on how well you are able and willing to set policies based on your own goals; how well you are able to identify those strategies that fit within the policies; and, most of all, how disciplined you are in staying with the course you have set for yourself.

With options, perhaps more than with most forms of investing, the establishment of intelligent policies is critical. There are so many different ways to use options, from highly speculative to highly conservative, that you need to know yourself quite thoroughly, and be able to follow your own specific policies. Most important among these policies is the definition of acceptable risks. Your personal risk standards reveal what forms of option investing, if any, will fit your portfolio and your financial plan. Perhaps they fit today but will not fit tomorrow. Perhaps the reverse is true.

Options might provide you with a very convenient form of diversification, protection, or income—or all of these benefits in various forms. But first, you need to decide what type of investor you are, and what type of investor you would like to be in the future.

If you are a speculator, you will favor income opportunities in the short term, and will have little permanent interest in the distant future. In this event, the higher risks will get your attention. Selling uncovered options or buying near-expiration, cheap positions will be especially appealing. As a speculator, you will also gravitate toward spreads and straddles for profit potential with minimum exposure to large losses. If you are a speculator in your stock portfolio, you may also want to use options to offset potential losses. For example, you might buy puts as protection against short sale losses.

If you are conservative and seek income rather than long-term growth, you can achieve a consistently high rate of return using covered calls. To protect the value of long positions, very conservative investors may also buy puts. This gives you downside protection without risking exercise. The put serves as a form of insurance, while covered calls provide immediate income and a higher than average rate of return—without the types of risk usually associated with options.

KNOWING THE RANGE OF RISK

Options serve the entire spectrum of risk profiles and can be used to speculate or to insure the value of stock. In order to identify how options can best serve your personal investing requirements, you must take three steps.

1. Become thoroughly aware of the various types of option investing. Before actually taking positions in options, prepare hypothetical variations and see how you do. Track options through the financial news and become familiar with options quotations and how they change from day to day.

2. Identify your personal investing and risk policies and set standards for yourself. Based on the goals you have devised as part of your financial plan, limit your market activity to actions that fit your policies.

3. Identify and understand the specific risks of options in each form and position, including contingent risks beyond unexpected movement in the price of the underlying stock. Avoid the trap of a simplistic point of view. Instead, develop a deeper sense of the options market.

The obvious risk for any option position is that the underlying stock will move in a direction opposite from what you expect. This danger is accepted by the speculator who seeks immediate income and by the conservative investor who uses options to lock in a rate of return or to insure the value of a position.

Beyond these, six other forms of risk must be acknowledged by every option investor: margin, personal goal, unavailability of a market, disruption in trading, brokerage, and commission risks.

Margin Risks

Most investors think of margin investing as buying stocks on credit. But in the options market, the margin requirement is different. Your broker will require that any short position in options must be protected with collateral.

Cash or securities must be deposited to protect a portion of the value when you assume a short position. For example, an investor who sells uncovered calls will be required to maintain a specific level of value in the brokerage account. The balance is at risk. So if the stock's value increases, the margin requirement will increase as well.

The risk is that in the event of unexpected changes in value of the underlying stock, you will be required to deposit additional money or securities to meet the margin requirement. Before entering into a position involving uncovered calls or puts, spreads, or straddles, you should discuss margin requirements with your broker and be certain that you can afford to meet those requirements.

Personal Goal Risks

You must set investing standards for yourself and establish rules you will follow consistently. If you do not take this step, your chances for profits from option trading will be reduced.

Example: You establish a number of goals and then set policies for yourself. One of your investing policies states that you will use no more than 15 percent of your portfolio's value to speculate in options. You begin a program of buying calls and puts and, over time, you earn a respectable profit. Then, unexpectedly, the market reverses its trend and you lose a large sum of money. In review, you discover that you had about 30 percent of your portfolio invested in options, and your losses are far higher than the level you were willing to accept. Somewhere along the way, you lost sight of your policy. You lost more than you were willing to have at risk because you forgot to monitor your portfolio.

Your standards should include identifying the point where you will close an open position. Avoid breaking your own rules by delaying action in the hope for greater profits in the future. Establish two points: *minimum gain* and *maximum loss*. When either point is reached, close your positions.

Unavailability of a Market Risk

A discussion of any option strategy assumes that you will be able to open and close positions whenever you want. Timing is the essential element of all option trades. But as an option investor, you must accept the continuous risk that a market could be unavailable for a number of reasons.

Example: On October 19, 1987, the stock market experienced the worst decline to that point in its history. Volume exceeded 600 million shares, and brokerage firms fell several days behind in completing orders. Investors were unable to reach their brokers by telephone, and even orders already placed were delayed several days. During the following week, prices of stocks moved through a wide range of values. Option investors, notably speculators, suffered tremendous losses in many instances. And they were unable to cut their losses by immediately placing a closing transaction—the market was not available.

The same problem can occur if an exchange halts trading options on a particular stock or ceases trading options altogether for a period of days. The exchanges cannot guarantee a prompt and continuous market.

Disruption in Trading Risks

Another risk is that trading will be halted in the underlying stock. When that occurs, trading in related options will also be halted. This situation presents a particularly severe risk for speculators.

Example: You sold an uncovered call last month and were paid a premium of 11 ($1100). Your strategy is to close out the position if the stock rises by 8 points or more, or to hold the position until expiration. But yesterday, a tender offer was made for the company at a price per share about $20 above current market value. You immediately called your broker to cancel your position. But you were told that the exchange halted trading in the stock, so you were not able to escape from your position. Now you realize that when trading is reactivated, the option will probably open 20 points higher. Your call will most likely be exercised.

In the same circumstances, a call buyer will not be able to close a position and take profits until trading is resumed. By that time, the rumor might have been denied, and the underlying stock's value could be back where it started.

In some situations, option buyers will be able to exercise even when trading has been halted. But in such circumstances, you will have to exercise without knowing the value of the underlying stock.

Brokerage Risks

If your brokerage firm becomes insolvent or if a regulatory agency takes over operation, you might be unable to close open positions at will. Or your positions might be closed without your authorization to eliminate risks of losses to the firm itself.

In the event of widespread brokerage insolvency, the Options Clearing Corporation would not necessarily be able to honor the exercise of all option contracts. The system of margin requirements and limitations on individual option positions in effect limits this risk. But every option investor must recognize that it exists.

Another form of brokerage risk involves the conduct of your personal broker. You should never grant unlimited trading discretion to a broker, no matter how much trust you have. Option trading, with its varied and special risks, is not appropriate in every form for every investor. There have been incidents of broker abuse in the past, and there probably will be again in the future. Unfortunately, when too much trust is placed in a broker, the problem is not discovered until after losses have occurred. It's a mistake to allow a broker, by virtue of experience or knowledge, to dictate positions in options or any other security without your consent and outside of your control.

Commission Risks

A calculated profit zone must be reduced to allow for the cost of trading. And a loss zone must be expanded for the same reason. Trading single options reduces the amount of money at risk, but also increases the per-option cost.

You risk losing sight of the cost of trading, so that marginally profitable trades on a precommission basis actually result in small losses. For the overall risk assumed, you might realize little or nothing for your efforts. Always calculate the risk and potential for profit with trading costs in mind.

EVALUATING YOUR RISK TOLERANCE

Every investor has a specific level of risk tolerance, or ability and willingness to accept risks. The degree of tolerance depends on a number of factors.

1. The amount of investment capital you have and are willing to spend on speculative positions—especially when the possibility of loss is high.

2. Your age, income level, and economic status, all of which affect your ability to tolerate risk.

3. Your experience and knowledge concerning the market and, specifically, the risks involved with a particular type of investment. Options, for example, are considered a highly specialized form of investing; a broker is required to ascertain your level of knowledge before allowing you to buy or sell any options.

4. The type of account in which you plan to trade. For example, if you are involved with options through an IRA or Keogh account, you probably can only sell covered calls. Most other strategies will not be allowed. Some custodians allow their self-directed retirement account holders to buy puts to hedge a position in certain cases. But you will not be allowed to speculate in options for your retirement account.

5. Your personal objectives. These include: the desire to conserve capital value; short-term maximum income; consistent rate of return; long-term growth; or a split among two or more objectives.

Some investors split their portfolios into distinct segments. One part is left in long-term growth investments, while another is put into more aggressive income funds or stocks. A small portion might be used for more speculative investments such as the purchase of options.

Whatever profile fits you, it should be well understood before any investment is made. Rather than depending on the advice of a broker, the financial rumors or news you read in the paper, or other isolated indicators and trends, be sure you invest with your risk tolerance in mind. That should be the force that guides every decision you make as an investor.

The best decisions are those made after evaluating risks. By putting down on paper the types of available option trades, you will gain a clear view of how options can fit into your portfolio. The evaluation process will also help you to avoid including options when they are not appropriate, given the risk tolerance you assign to yourself.

The risk evaluation worksheet for option investing shown in Table 9.1 will help you to classify options in categories of risk.

Table 9.1.   Risk Evaluation Worksheet

Lowest possible risk
_____ Covered call writing
_____ Put purchase for insurance (long position)
_____ Call purchase for insurance (short position)

Medium risk
_____ Ratio writing
_____ Combined strategies
_____ long _____ short

High risk
_____ Uncovered call writing
_____ Combined strategies
_____ long _____ short
_____ Call purchases for income
_____ Put purchases for income

Applying Limits

Awareness of your own limits must guide all option activities in your portfolio. Whenever you hold an open position, you must understand not only your goal and risk tolerance, but also the target rate of return you expect—or the degree of loss you are willing to accept.

To define these limits, identify option trades you will make by the rate of return and features of the option. For example, covered call sellers should always identify the potential return in selling calls if the stock is unchanged and if the option is exercised.

Option purchasers should evaluate what they will buy on these points.

1. *Maximum time value.* As a standard, buy only those options whose premiums do not contain an excessive level of time value. Time works against you as a buyer, and all of the time value will disappear by expiration date.

Example: You set a limit for yourself that options you buy should never contain more than 50 percent time value. So if you like a particular option and its premium is 4 ($400), your policy is that time value cannot be greater than 2 points; therefore, the option—because of your limit—can never be further from the striking price than the remaining 50 percent intrinsic value. In this case, that means 2 points.

2. *Time until expiration.* Buyers of very short-term options will be fortunate to realize a profit. That depends on enough movement in the underlying stock to increase intrinsic value of the call or put. So you need some time in order to build intrinsic profits. Decide in advance how many months you consider "ideal": enough time to allow for price movement, but not so much that you pay for an excessive level of time value.

Example: You would like to have the least amount of time value premium possible in options you buy. You also would like no less than two months until the expiration date. You set a limit that you will not even consider any options that will expire in the next two months.

3. *Number of options.* You must also decide how many options to buy in one trade. If you buy several contracts, the commission cost is greatly reduced, but if the move is not profitable, you also stand to lose more money.

Example: The fee for trading options with one discount broker for trades of $2000 or less is $18 plus 1.8 percent of the premium. Cost varies depending on the number of options traded at one time:

- One option, premium of 3 ($300) $23.40
- Two options, premium of 3 ($600) $28.80
- Three options, premium of 3 ($900) $34.20

For three options, the commission cost is $11.40 per contract or less than half the fee for a single contract.

4. *Target rate of return.* Enter every option trade with a goal for the rate of return. Identify this goal in advance.

Example: You have been buying options with the goal of making a 50 percent profit. You are willing to risk 100 percent losses if you don't achieve your goal, and you do reduce this goal when expiration approaches. Last month, you bought an option and paid a premium of 4 ($400). As of yesterday, the premium value had jumped to 6 ($600). You sold because your goal was reached.

5. *Buy and sell levels.* Along with a target rate of return, identify the premium level at which you will close the position. Respect this level. When premiums rise (for long positions) or fall (for short positions) to your target price, close the position. And, to minimize losses, also close if you reach an identified bail-out point.

Example: You usually buy options in groupings of three. You avoid any options with premiums above 3 ($300), so that you don't spend more than $900 on any one decision. You also set the standard that you will set within a specific price/value range. If the value of each option increases to $450 or more, you will sell. If the value of each option decreases to $150, you will also sell.

By identifying all of the features you consider minimally acceptable and all of the risks you are willing to assume, you then are able to select those options that fit your limits. If your limits are unrealistic, no options will be available.

Example: You have set a policy for yourself that incorporates several features. You have decided that options you will buy should never contain more than 25 percent time value in the total premium; they must have four months or more until expiration; and they must currently be in the money. However, when you try to apply this combined policy, you are unable to locate any options that meet all of the tests. You realize that, somewhere in the total configuration, you will need to make an adjustment.

When considering an option strategy, you should first calculate potential profits in the events of expiration and exercise and then set criteria for other points: maximum time value, time until expiration, number of contracts, target rate of return, and the price range in which you will sell. Use the option limits worksheet shown in Table 9.2 to set your limits. Then, respect the limits you set. By deciding in advance the characteristics of your option investment and by knowing when you will sell, you will avoid the common problem of in-

Table 9.2.   Option Limits

Covered Call Sale Criteria			
Rate of Return if Unchanged			
Dividends	$_____		
Call premium	_____	Total	$_____
		Cost of Stock	$_____
		Gain	_____%
Rate of Return if Exercised			
Dividends	$_____		
Call premium	_____		
Stock gain	_____	Total	$_____
		Cost of stock	$_____
		Gain	_____%
Option Purchase Criteria			

Maximum time value: _____%
Time until expiration: _____ months
Number of options: _____ contracts
Target rate of return: _____%
Sell level: increase to $_____ or decrease to $_____

vesting in a void. Many people have invested wisely at first, only to fail by not closing their positions at the right moment.

LOOKING TO THE FUTURE

Besides setting immediate standards and goals for option strategies in your portfolio, set long-term investing policies. Then fit option strategies into those policies.

It's a mistake to open an option position on the advice of a broker or adviser without first considering how that fits into your long-term investing policy. Options must be used in an appropriate context.

Example: You have written your financial plan and identified what you would like to achieve in the immediate and long-term future. You are willing to assume risks considered low to moderate. So you invest all of your capital in shares of blue-chip companies. In order to increase portfolio values over time, you consider one of two additional policies.

Policy 1: Hold the shares of stock as long-term investments. After many years, the accumulation of well-selected companies will increase the value of the investments, and current dividends will provide income.

Policy 2: Increase the value of your portfolio by purchasing shares and writing covered calls. Income from (a) profitable turnover through exercise, (b) call premiums, and (c) ongoing dividends will all be reinvested in a growing number of shares with several blue-chip companies.

In this example, the rate of return with Policy 2 will be greater due to the consistently high yield from selling calls. The return includes a discount for the purchase price and an increase for the amount of cash available to invest.

The long-term goal of building a portfolio's value can be achieved by using options in an appropriate way. You will give up the yields that might be earned if a company's stock jumps unexpectedly in value because selling calls locks in a striking price. But remembering that the goal is steady long-term growth, anticipating the possibility of sudden price swings is not applicable in either Policy 1 or Policy 2.

An impatient investor might be tempted to take a speculative approach, perhaps by buying options instead of stock. If the options are consistently profitable, you could achieve the goal of increasing value in a few months instead of having to wait several years. But the chances of loss are high, and this approach is contrary to your long-term goals.

All forms of investing contain special opportunities and problems. Options can be used to help reach your goals, address your risk tolerances, and even to protect yourself against losses. You may hedge positions, discount the prices you pay for stocks, or simply devote a small portion of your portfolio for pure speculation.

Those investors who do lose consistently in the options market share common characteristics. They fail to set goals and select strategies in their own best interests—usually because they have not taken the time to define their best interests. Their intentions are unclear, so they cannot possibly know when or how to buy and sell.

If you want to be among those investors who consistently profit in the options market, a different approach is needed. Success is haphazard if you go for it unprepared. But it is predictable and controllable if you first gain the knowledge, do the specific research, and apply the discipline demanded of this market. To some extent, you also need to experiment, to find out what it really is like to be in a particular position in the options market. Without actually committing funds and being at risk, you won't know what it feels like, even if you have worked it all out on paper.

It is a rewarding experience to devise a strategy, learn what you need to know to see it clearly, and then execute it successfully. You can profit from a well-planned and appropriate use of options. You can also enjoy the satisfaction that comes from mastering a complex investment and realizing that you are completely and totally in control.

Glossary

assignment   the act of exercise against a seller (When the buyer exercises an option, it is assigned to a seller, usually on a random basis.)

at the money   a condition in which the market value of the underlying security is identical to the striking price of the option

automatic exercise   action taken by the Options Clearing Corporation at the time of expiration, when an in-the-money option has not been otherwise exercised or canceled

average down   a technique for absorbing paper losses on stock investments (By buying shares periodically, the average price is higher than current market value, but part of the paper loss is absorbed on average, thereby enabling covered call writers to profit even when the stock has declined in value.)

average up   a technique for buying stocks when the market value is increasing (By buying shares periodically, the average price is consistently lower than current market value, thereby enabling the covered call writer to sell in-the-money calls when the overall basis in stock is lower than a desirable striking price.)

bear spread   the purchase and sale of calls or puts that will create maximum profits when the value of the underlying security falls (Options with a higher striking price are bought, and an equal number of options with a lower striking price are sold.)

buy 100 shares per month:

MONTH	PRICE	AVERAGE
Jan	$40	$40
Feb	38	39
Mar	36	38
Apr	34	37
May	27	35
Jun	29	34

Figure G.1.   Average down.

buy 100 shares per month:

MONTH	PRICE	AVERAGE
Jan	$40	$40
Feb	44	42
Mar	45	43
Apr	47	44
May	54	46
Jun	52	47

Figure G.2.   Average up.

beta   a measurement of the relative volatility of a stock, made by comparing the degree of price movement to movement in an overall index

box spread   the opening of a bull spread and a bear spread at the same time and on the same underlying stock (The investor will maximize profits when the stock rises or falls in value.)

break-even price   (also called break-even point) the price of the underlying stock at which the option investor breaks even (For the call buyer, this price amounts to the number of points above the striking price of the stock that equals the price of the call before allowing for commission costs.)

bull spread   the purchase and sale of calls or puts that will create maximum profits when the value of the underlying security rises

(Options with a lower striking price are bought, and an equal number of options with a higher striking price are sold.)

butterfly spread   the opening of positions in one striking price range and offsetting them with transactions at higher and lower ranges (For example, two calls are sold while another is purchased with a higher striking price and another is purchased with a lower striking price. The buy/sell decision can be reversed, and the strategy can involve either calls or puts.)

buyer   an investor who purchases a call or a put option (If the value of the option rises, the buyer will realize a profit by selling the option at a price above the purchase price.)

calendar spread   a strategy in which options bought and sold on the same underlying stock have different expiration dates

call   an option acquired by a buyer or granted by a seller to buy 100 shares of stock at a fixed price

called away   the result of having stock assigned (For each call option exercised, 100 shares of the seller's stock are called away at the striking price.)

class   all options traded on a single underlying security, including different striking prices and expiration dates

closed position   the status of an option that has been canceled or exercised or is expired

closing purchase transaction   a purchase to close a previous short position (For example, if you previously sold an option, a closing purchase transaction cancels that position.)

closing sale transaction   a sale to close a previous long position (For example, if you previously bought an option, a closing sale transaction cancels that position.)

combination   any multiple purchase and/or sale of related securities whose terms are not identical

contract   a single option, including the attributes of that option: identification of the stock on which it is written, the cost of the option, date the option will expire, and the fixed price at which the stock will be bought or sold if the option is exercised

conversion   the process of moving assigned stock from the seller of a call option or to the seller of a put option (Ownership is converted through the buyer's exercise of the option.)

cover   descriptive of the status when an investor is long in the stock and short in a call option (For each option contract sold, the investor owns 100 shares.)

covered option   a call option that is sold to create an open position, when the investor has 100 shares to cover the short option position

credit spread   any spread in which the receipts from short positions exceed the cost of long positions (For example, a May 40 call is sold for a premium of 6 and a May 45 call is bought for a premium of 1, with a net credit of 5 ($500) before commissions.)

current market value   the market value of stock at the present time

cycle   the series of expiration dates on the options of a particular underlying stock (There are three cycles, according to expiration dates: (1) January, April, July, and October; (2) February, May, August, and November; and (3) March, June, September, and December.)

debit spread   any spread in which the receipts from short positions are less than the cost of long positions (For example, a June 55 call is sold for a premium of 2 and a June 50 call is bought for a premium of 6, with a net debit of 4 ($400).)

deep in/deep out   terms describing an option when the underlying stock is more than 5 points above or 5 points below the striking price.

delivery   physical movement of stock from one owner to another (Shares are transferred upon registration of stock to the new owner and payment of the market value of those shares.)

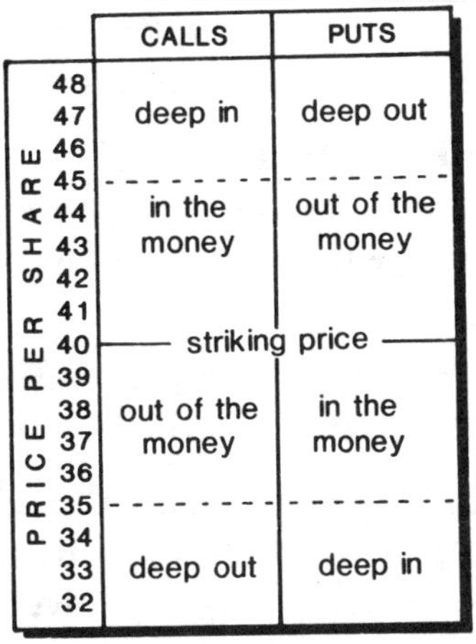

	CALLS	PUTS
48		
47	deep in	deep out
46		
45	- - - - - - -	- - - - - - -
44	in the	out of the
43	money	money
42		
41		
40	—— striking price ——	
39		
38	out of the	in the
37	money	money
36		
35	- - - - - - -	- - - - - - -
34		
33	deep out	deep in
32		

(left axis: SHARE PRICE — PER SHARE)

Figure G.3.   Deep in/deep out.

delta   the relationship of change in an option's premium to changes in the price of the underlying stock (When the two move the same number of points, the delta is 1.00; a higher or lower delta can act as a signal to take advantage of adjustments in time value.)

diagonal spread   a calendar spread in which the offsetting options have both different striking prices and different expiration dates

discount   a benefit of selling covered calls (The true price of the stock is reduced by the amount of premium received: If the basis

stock price change	OPTION PREMIUM CHANGE			
	1 point	2 points	3 points	4 points
1	1.00	2.00	3.00	4.00
2	0.50	1.00	1.50	2.00
3	0.33	0.67	1.00	1.33
4	0.25	0.50	0.75	1.00
5	0.20	0.40	0.60	0.80

Figure G.4.   Delta.

in stock is $30 per share and an option is sold for a premium of 5, the basis is discounted to $25 per share.)

downside protection   a strategy involving the purchase of one put for every 100 shares owned, as a form of insurance (Every point drop in the stock is matched by an increase of 1 point in the put.)

early exercise   the act of exercising an option prior to expiration date (Buyers have the right to exercise at any time.)

exercise   the act of buying or selling stock at the fixed price specified in the option contract (When a buyer exercises an option, he or she purchases stock at a price lower than market value; when a put is exercised, he or she sells stock at a price higher than market value.)

expiration date   the date that an option becomes worthless (Every option contract includes a specified date in the future on which it expires.)

expiration time   the latest possible time to place an order for cancellation or exercise, which is 5:30 P.M. (New York time) on the Friday immediately preceding the third Saturday of the expiration month

fundamental analysis   the study of financial aspects of a company or industry to determine the safety and value of an investment (Fundamentalists believe that future value is determined by historical profits, dividend yield, the P/E ratio, and other financial trends.)

hedge   a strategy in which one position protects the other (Buying a put is a form of hedge to protect the value of 100 shares of the underlying stock.)

horizontal spread   a calendar spread in which the offsetting options have the same striking price but different expiration dates

incremental return   a technique of avoiding exercise when the value of the underlying stock is rising (One call position is closed at a loss, but replaced by two or more new call positions; the net effect of this is to produce a cash profit.)

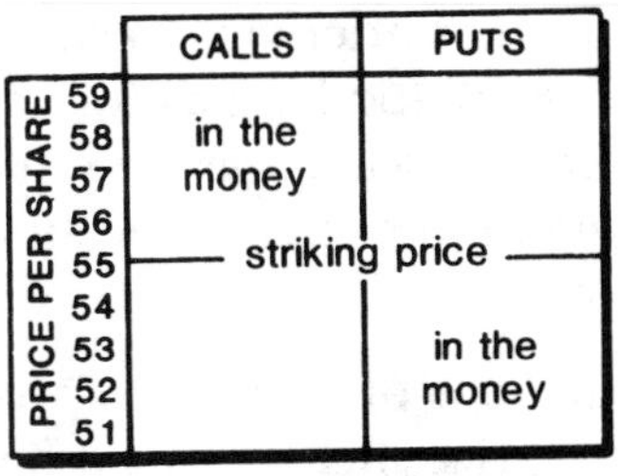

	CALLS	PUTS
59	in the	
58	money	
57		
56		
55	striking price	
54		
53		in the
52		money
51		

(PRICE PER SHARE)

Figure G.5.   In the money.

in the money   a condition in which the market value of the underlying stock is higher than the call's striking price or lower than the put's striking price

intrinsic value   the amount the option is in the money (An at-the-money or out-of-the-money option has no intrinsic value.)

last trading day   the Friday preceding the third Saturday of the expiration month of an option

leverage   the use of a limited amount of money to control greater values (A call buyer who spends $300 to control $5000 worth of stock has more leverage than an investor who spends $5000 to buy 100 shares.)

listed option   an option traded on a public exchange (Listed options are traded on the New York, Chicago, Pacific, American, and Philadelphia stock exchanges.)

STOCK VALUE	STRIKING PRICE	INTRINSIC VALUE
$38	$35	$3
43	45	0
41	40	1
65	65	0
21	20	1

Figure G.6.   Intrinsic value.

lock in   condition of the underlying security when the investor has an offsetting short call (So long as the call is open, the writer is locked into the striking price, regardless of current market value of the stock; in the event of exercise, the stock must be delivered at the locked-in price.)

long hedge   the purchase of options to protect a portfolio position in the event of a price increase, as a form of insurance (For example, an investor who is short 100 shares buys a call; if the stock's value rises, a corresponding rise in the call's premium will tend to offset losses.)

long position   the status of any investment that has been bought and is currently held, pending an offsetting sale (to cancel the position) or expiration

long straddle   the purchase of the same number of calls and puts with identical striking prices and expiration dates (This strategy will be profitable if the stock's price moves above or below the striking price to a degree greater than the total cost of buying options.)

loss zone   the price range of the underlying stock in which the option investor will lose (A limited loss occurs for a call buyer between the striking price and the break-even price; otherwise, the loss zone is any stock price lower than the option's striking price.)

margin   an account with a brokerage firm that contains a minimum, required amount of cash or securities to provide collateral for short positions or for purchases made and not paid for until sold

market value   the value of an investment as of a specified time or date, or the price that buyers are willing to pay and sellers are willing to receive for a stock or option

married put   descriptive of a hedge position when a put and 100 shares are bought at the same time (The put is "married" to the 100 shares on which the downside protection is provided.)

money spread   another term for vertical spread

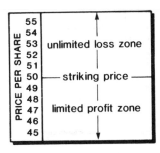

Figure G.7. Naked option.

naked option an option that is sold to create an open position, when the seller does not own 100 shares of the underlying stock

naked position the status when the seller does not own 100 shares of the underlying stock, but has sold a call

opening purchase transaction a transaction executed to buy, also known as "going long"

opening sale transaction a transaction executed to sell, also known as "going short"

open interest the number of open contracts on a particular option (Increases in open interest reflect the *total* contracts outstanding, but do not show whether volume is due to increased activity among buyers or sellers.)

open position the status when a purchase (long) transaction or a sale (short) transaction has been made (The position remains open until cancellation, expiration, or exercise.)

option the right to buy or sell 100 shares of stock at a fixed price and by a specified date

out of the money (the opposite of "in the money") a condition in which the market value of the underlying stock is lower than the call's striking price or higher than the put's striking price

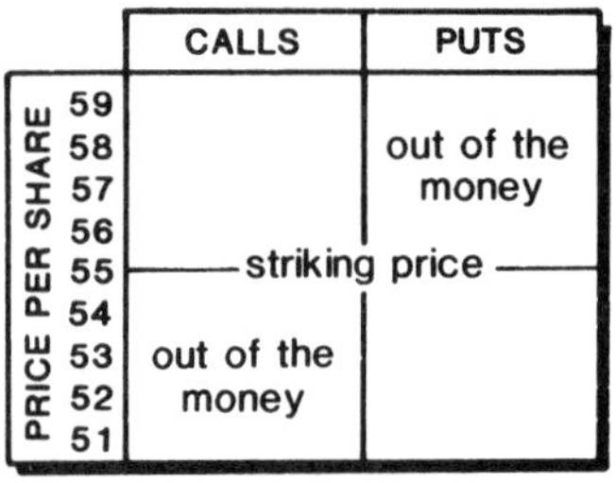

Figure G.8. Out of the money.

paper profits or losses (also called unrealized profits or losses) values that exist only because current market value is higher or lower than the investor's basis (These profits or losses can be realized—taken—only by closing the position.)

parity the condition of an option when the total premium is identical to intrinsic value and no time value exists

premium the current price of an option, which buyers pay and sellers receive at the time of the transaction (The amount is expressed as the amount per share, without dollar signs; for example, when a broker states that an option "is at 3," that means its premium is $300.)

profit zone the price range of the underlying stock in which the option investor will realize a profit (For a call buyer, the profit zone extends upward from the break-even price.)

put an option acquired by a buyer or granted by a seller to sell 100 shares of stock at a fixed price

put to seller the action that occurs when a put buyer exercises the put (The 100 shares of stock are sold—put—to the seller at the striking price.)

ratio calendar combination a spread strategy involving both a ratio between purchases and sales and a box spread (Long and short positions are opened in the same security but in varying numbers of contracts and with expiration dates extending over two or more periods in order to produce profits during periods of price increases or decreases in the underlying stock.)

ratio calendar spread   a strategy in which the number of options bought is different from the number sold and in which the expiration dates of the options on each side differ (This strategy establishes two profit/loss zones, one of which disappears upon the earlier expiration.)

ratio write   a relationship between long stock and short calls, other than one to one, that reduces risk on a portion of the total calls (For example, the owner of 400 shares sells five calls for a 5 to 4 ratio write involving four covered calls and one uncovered call, or 80 percent coverage of the entire position.)

realized profits or losses   profits or losses that are taken when an investor closes a position

return if exercised   the estimated rate of return an option seller will earn in the event of exercise (The calculation includes profit on the purchase and sale of the underlying stock, dividends, and premium received.)

return if unchanged   the estimated rate of return an option seller will earn if the option is not exercised (The assumption is that the stock will remain out of the money until expiration, so that the

exercise price 40
purchase price 38
May 40 call sold for 3
dividends earned $80

call premium	$300
dividend income	80
capital gain	200
return	$580
	15.3%

Figure G.9.   Return if exercised.

basis in stock $3800

sold May 40 call	$300
dividends earned	80
total	$380
return	10.0%

Figure G.10.   Return if unchanged.

return will consist of the call premium and any dividends earned on the underlying stock.)

reverse hedge   an extension of a long or short hedge in which more options are purchased than needed to provide insurance (For example, an investor is short 200 shares, and buys three calls; if the price rises, every 2 points of loss on the short stock position will be offset by 3 points of gain in the calls.)

roll down   the replacement of one call with another that has a lower striking price

roll forward   the replacement of one call with a call that has a higher striking price, but a later expiration date

roll up   the replacement of one call with a call that has a higher striking price

seller   an investor who sells an option (If the value of the option falls, the buyer will realize a profit by buying, or canceling, the option at a price below the original sales price.)

series   a group of options sharing identical terms

settlement date   the date on which an investor must pay for purchases or is paid for sales (Stock settlement occurs five business days after the transaction date; option settlement occurs on the business day following the transaction.)

short hedge   the purchase of options to protect a portfolio position in the event of a price decrease, as a form of insurance (For example, an investor who is long 100 shares buys a put; if the stock declines in value, the increased value of the put will tend to offset losses.)

short position   the status of any investment that has been sold and is currently held, pending an offsetting purchase (to cancel the position) or expiration

short straddle   the sale of the same number of calls and puts with identical striking prices and expiration dates (This strategy will be profitable if the stock's price does not move away from the striking price to a degree greater than the proceeds received by the investor.)

speculation   a risky use of money to create immediate or short-term profits, with the knowledge that substantial or total losses are also likely (Buying calls for leverage is a form of speculation: The buyer might earn a large profit in a short period of time or lose the entire premium.)

spread   the simultaneous purchase and sale of options—on the same underlying stock—with different striking prices or expiration dates or both (The purpose is to increase potential for profits, while reducing risks if the underlying stock's movement exceeds what is anticipated, or to take advantage of the timing of stock price movement.)

straddle   the simultaneous purchase and sale of the same number of calls and puts with identical striking prices and expiration dates

striking price   the price of stock indicated in the option contract (For example, when an option specifies a striking price of $45 per share, regardless of the actual market value of the stock, that option can be exercised at the striking price of $45 per share.)

suitability   a standard by which an investment or market strategy is judged (The investor's knowledge and experience in options is an important suitability standard, and a strategy is appropriate only if the investor can afford the risks that are involved.)

tax put   a strategy involving the sale of stock at a loss—taken for tax purposes—and the sale of a put (The premium on the put eliminates the loss on sale of stock: If exercised, the investor buys back the stock at the striking price.)

technical analysis   the study of trends and statistics in the market to identify buying and selling opportunities (Technicians believe that price movement is predictable based on historical patterns and trends.)

terms   the complete description of an option including the striking price, expiration month, type (call or put), and underlying security

time spread   another term for calendar spread

time value   the option's premium above any intrinsic value (When an option is at the money or out of the money, the entire premium represents time value.)

total return   the combination of income from the call premium, capital gains in the stock, and any dividends received (Total return should be computed in two ways: if the option is exercised and if it expires worthless.)

uncovered option   the same as a naked option, or the opposite of a covered option (when a call is sold and the investor also owns 100 shares)

TOTAL PREMIUM	INTRINSIC VALUE	TIME VALUE
$4	$3	$1
2	0	2
4	1	3
1	0	1
3	1	2

Figure G.11.   Time value.

stock exercised at
$40 (basis $34),
held for 13 months:

option premium	$ 800
dividends	110
capital gain	600
total	$1510
13 months	44.4%
annualized	41.0%

Figure G.12.   Total return.

underlying stock   (also called underlying security) the stock on which the option grants rights to buy or sell (Every stock option refers to a specific, underlying stock.)

variable hedge   a hedge between two related option positions, where one side involves more options than the other (For example, you buy three calls and sell one at a lower striking price. The difference in premium reduces the cost and might even result in cash proceeds, but the potential loss from the short call is offset by potential gains in the long calls.)

vertical spread   any bull or bear spread that involves options with different striking prices, but identical expiration dates

volatility   a measure of the degree of change in a stock's market price during a twelve-month period, stated as a percentage (To compute, subtract the lowest price from the highest price during the twelve months and divide the difference by the annual low, then multiply by 100.)

$$\frac{\text{high} - \text{low}}{\text{low}} = 100$$

volume   the level of trading activity in a stock, an option, or in the market as a whole

$$\boxed{\begin{array}{c} \text{high} - \text{low} \\ \hline \text{low} \end{array}}$$

ANNUAL HIGH	ANNUAL LOW	PERCENT
$ 65	$ 43	51%
37	34	9
45	41	10
35	25	4
84	62	35
71	68	4
118	101	17
154	112	38

Figure G.13.   Volatility.

wasting asset   any asset that will decline in value over time (An option is a wasting asset because it will be worth its intrinsic value on expiration day and worthless after expiration day.)

writer   the individual who sells—writes—a call

Index